FUTURIST ADVERTISING

FUTURIST ADVERTISING

A new solution for the future of advertising

Emanuele Nenna

Viva Books
New Delhi | Mumbai | Chennai | Kolkata
Bengaluru | Hyderabad | Kochi | Guwahati

First Indian Edition 2014

VIVA BOOKS PRIVATE LIMITED

- 4737/23 Ansari Road, Daryaganj, New Delhi 110 002
  E-mail: vivadelhi@vivagroupindia.net, Tel. 42242200
- 76, Service Industries, Shirvane, Sector 1, Nerul, Navi Mumbai 400 706
  E-mail: vivamumbai@vivagroupindia.net, Tel. 27721273, 27721274
- Megh Towers, Old No. 307, New No. 165, Poonamallee High Road, Maduravoyal
  Chennai - 600 095 E-mail: vivachennai@vivagroupindia.net, Tel. 23780991, 23780992
- B-103, Jindal Towers, 21/1A/3 Darga Road, Kolkata 700 017
  E-mail: vivakolkata@vivagroupindia.net, Tel. 22836381, 22816713
- 7, Sovereign Park Apartments, 56-58, K. R. Road, Basavanagudi, Bengaluru 560 004
  E-mail: vivabangalore@vivagroupindia.net, Tel. 26607409, 26607410
- 101-102 Mughal Marc Apartments, 3-4-637 to 641, Narayanguda, Hyderabad 500 029
  E-mail: vivahyderabad@vivagroupindia.net, Tel. 27564481, 27564482
- Beevi Towers, First Floor, SRM Road, Kaloor, Kochi 682 018, Kerala
  E-mail: vivakochi@vivagroupindia.net, Tel: 0484-2403055, 2403056
- 232, GNB Road, Beside UCO Bank, Silpukhuri, Guwahati 781 003
  E-mail: vivaguwahati@vivagroupindia.net, Tel: 0361-2666386

www.vivagroupindia.com

Published by arrangement with
LID Publishing
6-8, Underwood Street
London N1 7JQ
UK

ISBN : 978-81-309-2687-2

Published by Vinod Vasishtha for Viva Books Private Limited, 4737/23, Ansari Road, Daryaganj, New Delhi - 110 002.

Printed and bound by Saku Printing House, New Delhi.

To each
era its art,
to art its freedom.

Gustav Klimt

We are so busy measuring public opinion
that we forget we can mold it.
We are so busy listening to statistics
we forget we can create them.

Bill Bernbach

CONTENTS

Preface 9

Part I: The Preliminaries 13
Chapter 1: The Starting Point 15
Chapter 2: Revolution or Evolution? 23
Chapter 3: Portraits 31
Chapter 4: Back to Basics 39

Part 2: Multiplication 49
Chapter 5: The Two-Person Agency 51
Chapter 6: The Planner Trinity 67
Chapter 7: The Creative Duo is a Foursome. Plus One 79

Part 3: Creatives Today 93
Chapter 8: The Art Director Today 95
Chapter 9: Fresh from the States: the Idea Writer 105
Chapter 10: The Attention Planner 115
Chapter 11: The Digital Creative Planner 131
Chapter 12: The Consumer Turns Brainstormer: the "Creative Consumer" 139

Part 4: The End 147
Chapter 13: Long Live (Neutral) Advertising! 149

Acknowledgements 154

PREFACE

by Mark Tungate

One of my favourite movies is The Moderns. Directed by Alan Rudolph, it's about American nationals living in Paris in the 1920s. As a foreigner living in Paris (and a sucker for nostalgia), the chiaroscuro backdrop of that time and place has always appealed to me. The characters spend their time scribbling and scrapping in bars, listening to jazz music and flirting with avant-garde artists.

At the end of the film, one of the main characters decides to move on. To Hollywood, to be precise. "It's the future!" he exclaims. His best friend protests, "but I thought you said Paris was the future!"

His pal looks at him witheringly. "The future doesn't stay in one place." That's the problem with the future. It keeps shifting beneath your feet.

When I wrote a book called Adland a few years ago, it was clearly subtitled A Global History of Advertising. Note the use of the word "history".

It only featured one chapter on the future of advertising, right at the very end. I wasn't able to draw any definite conclusions because the digital revolution – or evolution, if you like – was just beginning. No-one knew what the future was going to be, least of all me.

To emphasize the point, I should specify that I wrote my book in 2006. Blogs were the height of fashion. I did not mention Facebook because I had barely heard of it (in fact, it only opened to the public that year). Twitter did not even exist and neither did the iPhone.

Not only is the future difficult to pin down – it also has a habit of arriving too soon. Science fiction writer William Gibson recently stopped writing books set in the future because by the time his ideas hit the page, they were already a reality.

If a future hi-tech guru – a man who made a career out of being a visionary and who coined the term “cyberspace” – finds it hard to keep up, then no wonder advertising agencies are struggling.

As you can imagine, I’m also a fan of Mad Men. Everybody seems to love this series set on the Madison Avenue of the early 1960s, particularly those in the field of advertising. I believe that this is partly because it portrays their industry at an earlier, less complicated time – an era so innocent that placing a tiny Volkswagen Beetle on an otherwise blank page seemed radical.

Entire families would sit down to watch their favourite TV show at the appointed hour. You could whoosh advertising into their brains like medicine into the mouths of babes.

As you are well aware, this is no longer the case and hasn’t been for a long time: audience fragmentation began with satellite TV and continued with the internet.

But this wasn’t widely reflected in the structure of

advertising agencies, which have remained frozen in the Mad Men era. Sure, some of them have hired digital people, but it's more like they're dabbling in the odd small-time solution – it is as though they were trying to bolt a shiny new body onto the chassis of a 1960s Volkswagen Beetle.

And digital people weren't the only thing they needed. In fact, the future would involve multi-platform storytelling. So they needed experts in product placement, design, licensing, merchandising and CRM ... all sitting around the same table ... with someone to coordinate the whole lot of them.

"Oh – and where are our media people? They're in a different company? How did that happen?"

For a few years the future seemed to taunt and assail the advertising industry, while remaining just out of its reach. Now, the situation I described earlier is coming to pass. Advertising agencies are mutating into something far richer and more complex than mere advertising agencies. After the violent tectonic shifts of the last decade, a new landscape is emerging.

The book you're now holding maps that landscape.

Emanuele Nenna was into digital logic long before it loomed so large in our lives. He didn't survive the earthquake: he read the patterns on the seismograph machine and acted accordingly.

This is his proposal for the perfect advertising agency of today ... and maybe even that of tomorrow.

PART 1
THE PRELIMINARIES

1

THE STARTING POINT

Once upon a time, snowboarding did not exist.

There was skiing, there was surfing and windsurfing, and there was skateboarding. Now the world's mountains are overrun with brightly coloured boards and well-equipped snow parks that are an increasingly common feature alongside the finest ski pistes. Snowboarding is on TV; it has its own world championships and world champions.

Nowadays it is all too natural to think of snowboarders as native to the sport: no-one asks the Olympic champion if he is a former skier, skateboarder or surfer. He likely began tackling pistes on his snowboard as a youngster. But take a short hop back to the seventies and eighties and you'll find yourself in an entirely different scenario. Back then no-one took up snowboarding from scratch because it was too new a sport and had no history of its own. There were no thoroughbred snowboarders, just athletes and sportsmen who were learning because, more than others, they had the potential to excel at that particular discipline.

The best ones, it is said, were the surfers. It may seem rather odd that people accustomed to Californian beaches and sunshine would have felt so at home on the freezing cold snow-covered peaks of Michigan, and yet it appears they were.

If we peruse the world snowboarding rankings today we'll see that the "snow factor" prevails over the "board factor", given that all the big names hail from the same lands that produce skiing champions: Austria, Scandinavia, Germany, Italy, France, Canada and the US ... but not California. Of course, this book isn't concerned with snowboarding topography. It is, however, concerned with observing how the world is changing; and just as sports evolve, so does advertising.

It all seems to point to the fact that advertising agencies and their clientele will have to compete on a snowboard track with their feet firmly on a board ... but there are still no professional snowboarders around. Skiers, surfers and skaters are trying to make their mark, and although champions in their own right, they are novices when it comes to taking on the new snowboard race routes.

The aim of the book you hold in your hands is to identify a new creative team that has what it takes to face today's advertising challenges. In order to explain their characteristics we have to resort to using the same old categories, the ones established by decades of history: art direction and copywriting. However, this will not always be the case.

My work will be a contribution to the cause. The theme of innovation is not new to me. Four years ago I began asking questions along these lines and wrote my first book on communication, Not Available: The ideal communication agency – How it should be and why it doesn't exist.

The initial observation was very clear: in 2007 there was a chasm, a void, which I described by comparing notes with other company-based marketing men. After the book I did more: I convinced two comrades-in-adventure to create an agency to occupy the void that remained unfilled by the lumbering leviathan international communication groups to give the market the answers it was searching for. We created Now Available, calling it so to ratify the novelty, the change in pace and the new perspective: the agency that clients were asking for but were unable to find during those years, when the shelves were full of the usual luxury ATL brands with a little too much dust on them and hundreds of private labels poor on credibility and professionalism.

In actual fact Now Available – Italy's first ever "neutral agency" – has done well: in just four years, after starting from scratch, it vaunts a rich and varied portfolio of clients and campaigns ranging from classic advertising to promotional projects, including social, digital and mobile advertising, developed for the likes of such high-profile brands as MTV, Nestlé, Volkswagen, Henkel, Che Banca! and Gazzetta dello Sport, all of whom have one thing in common: the ability to look ahead. With forty people and a steady rise in turnover it is, in short, a good agency, which has somehow forged an alternative route to the beaten track.

However, setting off in the right direction does not necessarily mean arriving at the right destination. Navigating means moving, asking questions, doing some soul-searching; going with the flow, the currents and the winds. If back in 2007 I felt there was a need for a new agency model, now I'm convinced that new professional figures are necessary to produce a new genre of creative thought.

To my mind Now Available is the ideal place in which to field-test original advertising solutions. Not around the table, but with real clients, products and consumers. It is the ideal setting in which to imagine and test future scenarios. When something takes on its own clear, distinct and seemingly linear shape, then it is time to write, establish concepts, propose theses, and submit ideas to the mercy of public opinion to see what effect they have.

I have taken up my pen again now because I have something new and interesting to tell.

Italy's great creative directors have only recently become

fully aware of the fact that everything is changing as they know it and that their model is inadequate because it is outdated, yet in many instances they are still failing to find a solution to the problem. Viewed from the outside, their attempt to react is admirable; so why are they unsuccessful?

They are unsuccessful for a variety of reasons. One: because it's hard. Even the few who have been working on new models and creative professions for years with dedication, vision, motivation and with very talented people have not yet succeeded in reaching a safe haven. Just imagine those who, in the early years, looked on, discussing which fake candidates to nominate for Cannes as they waited for the "bubble" of novelty to burst and thus remove the inconvenience.

Meanwhile, "the suits" in their respective agencies had to balance the books and found themselves having to fire all the senior art directors (the most expensive ones) and replace them with droves of cheap enthusiastic youngsters and inexperienced interns. (Note to the reader: from time to time I will allow myself to indulge in a little "polite" argument, but I will try not to go over the top. This book aims to discuss its own theory, not to challenge others.)

Two: because it's unprofitable. Or very expensive. Or both. Once upon a time all it took was intuition (or a stroke of genius, if you are among those who regard Bill Bernbach and David Ogilvy as geniuses), followed by superior execution, and there you had it. Things aren't like that now.

Today, behind every brand communication project lie a thousand different media (each with its own characteristics), an urgent need for specific knowledge (which can be expensive), and hours and hours of skilled human labour. And on the other side, there's a client – upon whom many agencies have had a negative influence – who instead of opening up the purse strings tightens them all the more, because an event cannot possibly cost more than billboarding, and a viral video cannot possibly cost more than a 30-second TV ad.

This is the economic paradox of the current system in Italy, just as it is in many other countries: advertising agencies are called on to produce advertising products that require many hours of work, but, as per the aforementioned advertising supermarket, they must be offered at an increasingly lower rate.

In these pages I shall refer to several "wizards" in the history of advertising. On the subject of the cost of advertising campaigns that are not very compatible with agency profits (or with the farsightedness of entrepreneurs), the frustration of Earnest Elmo Calking, a forerunner of Bernbach, comes to mind. It was around 1900 when he suggested to his boss (a certain Bates, but not "the" Bates) that he should invest in someone who was an expert in "images" – a graphic artist or draughtsman – to complement the copywriters. The reply was a firm no: production of that new type of advertising would have been decidedly more expensive and therefore not worth it.

Three (and last, but certainly not least): because the face of creativity today really is changing, and lots of agencies and art directors (and not just the "older" ones, believe me!) cannot understand this, or at least they pretend not to. Art directors and copywriters alone are no longer enough, however great, open-minded and ingenious they may be.

In 1949 Bernbach realized that art directors and copywriters would lead to great advertising campaigns if they were used together. Before then, it was the art director who created the campaign. All the copywriter did was to place his text in the blank space left for him by his colleague. Or – as was more often the case – good text would lead the way and the graphic artist on duty would create the layout. Since then no-one has ever questioned the delegation of a campaign to this creative duo. And this creative duo has become so consolidated that in recent years it has also changed the face of art direction, which (in Italy in particular) is left less in the hands of a single individual and increasingly entrusted to an art director and copywriter duo.

Without wishing to turn my back on how advertising has been conducted for the past sixty years, my theory is precisely this: nowadays two people are no longer enough to be able to create new-generation campaigns (that is, ones capable of performing the persuasive role that advertising has always had). We can no longer leave it to the skiers and surfers alone. A new means of creativity must be invented along with new professional figures to carry it out.

Here's the thing: a short while ago at the agency, someone (I know exactly who it was, but I won't name them) commented during one of many chats on the chief world systems and internal organizations, quite unaware of its expressive portent, that "the creative duo is a foursome". An excellent off-the-cuff effective synthesis, I think. So much so that I used this expression as the title for the original version of my book. Naturally, the number four concept is reflected in this new, international edition of the same book. Here, then, is the 4Cast: an attempt to "foursee" what's next, being sure that two is not enough.

Happy
reading.

2

REVOLUTION OR EVOLUTION?

I won't keep you on tenterhooks: it's evolution.

I'm convinced about this; so much so that I've based my theory on it. And in doing so, I've clashed with several of the clichés that dominate the current and future state of communication, which at times seem more like prophecies than debatable, sustainable thoughts.

I say "evolution" for one reason in particular: in spite of the wall of smoke fanned by a few new gurus (and by the silence of the old ones), the objective of advertising today remains the same as that of 150 years ago: to help client companies sell their products on the market. And creativity, which is its main element, must (or at least ought to) tailor itself to this function, as it always has done, simply by adapting to the times.

This book is about the changing face of advertising and I've no intention of playing down the extreme transformations that we are currently witnessing. However, at the same time – perhaps in slight countertrend – I prefer to speak of "evolution" while clinging to the main theme that links today's advertisers with those of yesteryear; a theme associated with the reason for the birth of advertising.

According to the definition of one of the founding fathers of this highly respectable field, John E. Kennedy, "advertising is salesmanship-in-print". At that time advertising only ever appeared in print (then evolution brought with it posters, radio, TV and cinema). Today advertising is salesmanship-in-whatever, but it is still nonetheless all about the ability to sell.

This is not the place for retracing advertising history from its origins: there are already some first-rate books on that subject. I'll just limit myself to naming a few prominent names to go with my observations. For the moment, what matters to me most is to show, by calling on Lasker, Hopkins, Reeves and other witnesses, that advertising has always been associated with marketing.

The great advertising campaigns of the past are remembered as much for their creative aspect as for the successful sales they generated. We all feel in some way that we are the heirs and disciples of the creative revolution attributed to Bernbach, but if "think small" hadn't convinced the Americans (or some of them at least) to review their idea of the kind of car they were willing to drive (and purchase), it probably wouldn't be the all-time most cited campaign at advertising schools that it is now.

If the Marlboro cowboy hadn't made the cigarette brand number one in the world (before he came along, the cigarettes had been known as a "ladies brand"), perhaps the legend of Leo Burnett would not have survived into our era. In the history of advertising, every "advertising legend" has given his/her own slant: there have been those who were more devoted to research and to the scientific nature of the message and those who relied more on talent and sheer creativity. However, the success of a campaign for all concerned, in any era, has always been the client companies' sales curves (and there's nothing artistic about those).

Many who talk of revolution in reference to the current changes in our profession are often denying a continuity with this interpretation of advertising. I've recently read several books by Italian and international authors (sheer cowardice prevents me from naming them) who openly discuss new models and rules while condemning the old ones to the gallows, as well as new roles for advertising companies, and thus for advertisers as well. Many of the new gurus (those most able to entrance audiences from their modern upholstered pulpits) use phrases like "today marketing isn't made by companies, but rather by consumers" or "once upon a time advertising was used for the purpose of selling, now it's used for evangelizing".

The famous *Cluetrain Manifesto,* an unequivocal distancing from the advertising of yesteryear, is certainly rich in interesting new assertions; however, if these are read with revenge in mind, they may be interpreted in an extremely unrealistic manner. Those who champion the revolution implicitly prophesy that "the new" will sweep away the old. This is not what we are witnessing at all. The new supports, improves and complements the old, and sometimes even replaces it. It does not necessarily renounce it.

If you talk of new media and languages, I'm the first one to get excited and feel a part of it. However, at the same time I think that hailing new-generation communication as "revolutionary" is something that threatens to undermine the future of advertising if the "old" assumptions that engender new ideas are repudiated.

It is true that today many spenders allow themselves to be inveigled by new forms of communication without asking too many questions about their actual efficacy in terms of return for their company (also because, in terms of percentage, the budget allocated to these pursuits is often laughable). Of course, if a certain kind of approach is fashionable, one cannot fail to join in the party, one cannot lag behind – who would deny themselves a nice little *flash mob*? Fine, there's absolutely no harm in going along with the trends a little – it does everyone good, clients and creative designers alike. You experiment, try out new things, you even learn from your mistakes (or from getting things right through lucky guesses). However, if advertising today expects to be able to survive on this alone, then it won't be around for much longer. If modern advertising wishes to emancipate itself from the old by repudiating its logic and sense in the name of quasi-subversive concepts (which we will examine shortly), it will soon find itself trapped at a dead end.

Here's a question for you: why is it that today in Italy, in 2012, over 50% of many budgets is still being invested in television (and over 80% in classic media)? Please don't answer with something like "because Italy has always been a little behind the times". The reason is another: if companies are spending their money on television it is because television is still alive and often more effective than other media (though increasingly less so, as I'm sure we'll all agree). The future does not seem to hold any Bastille Day when good old TV will be axed.

Languages change, consumer goods change, people change. Society evolves and with it its media. Nowadays all this happens faster than ever before. So, woe betide those who remain on the blocks, woe betide those who fail to notice in time and lose ground. However, at the same time let us professionals in the trade take care not to cut the umbilical cord that ties us to our advertising origins. For it is the same cord that ties us to our clients: our mission is to contribute to their commercial success using our ideas and professionalism. The success of our agencies will depend on theirs.

On this subject here's a fitting anecdote concerning one Claude Hopkins. If you are in advertising, you're bound to know all about him. If, however, you do not know who he is, don't worry; you will be hearing of him a great deal in these pages, for Hopkins is one of my heroes. Anyway, he's a pre-Bernbach advertiser (his autobiography, *My Life in Advertising*, dates back to 1927!). Hopkins was working on an advertising campaign for Pepsodent and – being the scrupulous product expert that he was – discovered that the product he was writing about was capable of fighting tooth plaque (the first such product in the world).

Obviously, no-one even knew what plaque was because no-one had ever heard of it.! He did the campaign and, convinced as he was of the efficacy (and purport) of his advertising intuition, he purchased a share in the company. You can imagine the happy outcome: Pepsodent rocketed, as did Hopkins' wealth. Good story, eh? In any case, we'll be returning to the concept of the client-advertiser partnership later on.

Having finished with the philological (and philosophical) theme launched in this chapter, there remains the central theme: the real aim of this book. Although not exactly a bloody revolution, the change in advertising is underway, or rather, has become a necessity. And now is the time to address it seriously, to find the right way for its evolution to develop; something that no-one seems to have illustrated clearly, but which I think now, at long last, can be outlined with an element of certainty.

Creative thought, creative professionals and advertising agencies all have to evolve. But in which direction? If you have paid money to buy this book it is only fair that I should try to give you an answer.

In the next chapter you will read all about cases that have arisen in advertising offices in recent months. These will help me to illustrate that there is very broad scope for the evolution of the advertiser species, both to help us identify and avoid the song of several modern sirens.

3

PORTRAITS

Portrait of an EACR (Evolved Anachronistic Creative Reactionary)

He's not so much old as incredibly stale. A few witty (and modern) T-shirts attempt to belie his conservative nature. He has a favourite saying on the centrality of the idea. "An idea is an idea. If it's good it will work on any platform." Only he can come up with the idea (the Big Idea, of course, with a capital "B" and "I". He is The Creative One.

Then someone else will decline the idea (yes, "decline" he term we use!). He is not an art director because he is still too young (on paper, that is). However, if the right opportunity comes along he soon will be, bringing with him a breath of fresh air in an advertising world increasingly run by incompetent CEOs and ignorant clients. (Do not tell him that one of his predecessors, one slightly more famous than him, said that there was no such thing as a bad client. He will reply: Jerry who?).

Yes, it is an outrage that the decision maker in a business in which creativity is paramount is not a creative person, or is a mediocre creative person who has never won an award at Cannes. How can the big spenders fail to understand that this is a task for someone of his calibre and not for "suits" with all their figures and business plans? But he is confident that as soon as he gets the chance he will bring light and distinction to a profession that has fallen into decline.

It is in decline because clients are cutting their budgets: they won't let you use the most expensive photographers, and more importantly, they are ignoramuses. They speak a totally different language to creatives. They are incapable of drafting a brief. They are not interested in who wins the Clio. They do not realize that still today (and who knows for how much longer) the real art of advertising can be seen in the big films.

When his turn comes he will be the one who selects the brands to work with and will force his ad campaigns on them. For it is the task of the creative person to create winning campaigns without all the obstacles, tests and surveys ordered by the client's marketing people. And it should be left to the account planners (or at least to the CEOs, who see the account planners as insignificant) to refuse to follow the client's instructions, because the client doesn't know what he's talking about and has to be educated and coerced.

Later, the client will be grateful to the agency. And if the client isn't grateful, then the client will know where to go – the market is full of third-rate agencies willing to do anything for a few thousand Euro. He will have his team of heavily salaried whiz-kids (because you have to pay for talent) and under him a legion of interns who will be grateful to him every day for the opportunities he gives them. Young, motivated and vying with one another so that the right ones come out on top.

After all, he too was once treated like that. It takes blood, sweat and tears to enter the realm of the Creative Gods. It's not that easy and it's not for the faint-hearted. And as for new methods of communication, he can't see what the problem is. Sure, he's never had to devise an event, but if it's just a question of coming up with an idea, who better than him to do it? Those who work at events agencies aren't creatives! Give him the name of a leading creative from the world of events, digital or direct marketing. You can't? That's because there are no names and no talent there. Creativity does not reside in that field, even if today, in order to save money, clients have their campaigns devised by "those below".

But then, where is all this novelty anyway? Isn't "ambient" the new outdoor format? (Yes, he likes the "ambient" genre, just as he likes referring to any kind of communication that falls outside his standard models as "ambient".) He likes guerrilla marketing as well – indeed, he takes it literally: his ideas are "explosive". If he wants to get noticed he has to do things in a big way, perhaps by changing road signs or something similar.

But the clients just don't get him: they ask for big ideas then get scared by any old motorway pile-up. And the internet? Sure, it's an expanding medium – any self-respecting media mix cannot do without it (that's what he says, but he doesn't believe it for a minute: who ever clicks on a banner or opens a direct email?) And if it is explained to him that the web is more than this, he just doesn't listen, because he already knows. They don't have to explain anything to him, he who is able to quote two or three case histories that won awards at Cannes.

Of course, he's careful not to be caught out as he proudly confides to a colleague that he's not on Facebook and still hasn't understood exactly what Twitter is all about – which, in his opinion, is for time-wasting people hooked on this stuff. At the end of the day, all you need to do is to take on four big kids brought up on bread and social networks as interns: they'll take care of adding all the useless IT frills that the clients like so much.

Perhaps in the meantime he could go on a shopping trip

to the most interesting web agencies with a view to hiring a few digital experts. It won't be difficult to convince a few "webbers" to join his team: if they are True Creatives, then even if they hail from the digital world they will be able to recognize the Right Path. He will ask his boss for a budget and will hire a whole team of experts. That way, not even that problem will exist. There's even a room vacant on the floor below now, what with all the laying off going on in this period. Sure, seeing all the great and legendary advertising agencies limping along is a truly sad sight. But that's the way it has to be. Progress. Perhaps things were better when they were worse ...

Portrait of the NWIYI (Naïve, Well-Intentioned Young Innovator)

The fact that this person is well-meaning, since he is driven by noble ideals, makes this character a more likeable fellow, though we still cannot include him among the "goodies" in this story. He is naïve, as young men often are, but does not know it. This is why he may seem presumptuous.

For he has the truth in his pocket; the kind that only a young man such as he could have, because he remains uninfluenced by the dogmas of traditional advertising, the bad kind that bamboozled the masses and convinced them to buy products which, at best, were unnecessary and at worst plagiarized behaviours and consumption through subtle manipulatory forms.

Only those able to escape the dictates of TV are fully justified in speaking of innovation. Only he can understand how people today think. He is allergic to many words of the ancien régime, words like "consumers" or "target", which he sees as veritable insults. We are dealing with people here, not targets. "People are no longer stupid". Those in marketing, and especially those in advertising, who still persist in using such words, are deemed archaic beings who are certainly incapable of treading the boards of the modern communication scenario.

However, beware: avoiding antiquated and hence taboo words, those censured by the advance of the new, is not enough. In particular, one should also beware of the most recent terms. If he hears someone speaking enthusiastically of smart mobs he reproaches him by saying that they are passé. A social network that ends up a mass affair is doomed to failure, superseded by what we do not yet know. He is superficial. He cites international case histories left, right and centre, but hopes that no-one will ask him any questions because he wouldn't know how to reply. Just like the disciple of a new religion, he doesn't ask himself many questions.

If his gurus have spoken well of a brand, then that's a good brand. If they have spoken badly of it, then that brand has had it. He criticizes current advertising schemes without knowing anything about them. He quotes Bernbach because he has been told by many that he was a giant in advertising, but in actual fact he really hasn't the foggiest who he was, beyond perhaps the copywriter for Volkswagen and Avis, and the "B" in DDB. He feels that the future of communication lies in his hands, but he has never studied the past.

He is well aware of the latest influences on public opinion and believes that they are his friends. He still hasn't realized that the best, most followed bloggers have become publishers and sell advertising space, or else are paid writers like the much-loathed journalists in someone's pay. Or maybe he does know, but he makes a whole load of distinctions to defend the field. He thinks that one good idea can singlehandedly reach millions and millions of people, yet rejoices when 34 bloggers subscribe to a brand's idea.

He is the one who can outline brand communication strategies because he speaks the new lingos and knows all the hidden pitfalls of brands in the fantastic realm of sharing and exchanging ideas and co-creating. For example, he knows of the potential "boomerang effect" of certain contrivances in advertising (oh, and how he relishes using that term!), while the ignorant client does not know (here the naïve innovator is much like the reactionary creative in his appraisal of the client). He fears a negative post on Facebook more than a bad review in the Corriere della Sera.

However, in the end, we have said that he's a great idealist: the good brands (the ones that do what consumers – sorry, I mean, "people" – expect of them) will triumph over the lesser brands, and the world will be a better place where companies and consumers (or rather, people who buy and use the goods produced by those companies) will be on the same level, with the same rights and duties. And perhaps, while we're at it, there will be no more injustice or war either.

The Portrait of a Modern Sage

"I really believe
in the power
of advertising.
But I believe in the
power of advertising that's
in synch with what
consumers want."

– *David Droga*

4

BACK TO BASICS

I began this book by talking about my opposition to the term "revolution", a word commonly perceived to refer to concepts of severance, a complete change of direction, subversion, and disownment of the status quo, which poses more of a threat than a help to the modernization cause. However, after researching Latinist memoirs I find yet another meaning for the term: an etymological interpretation of "revolution" leads me to "return"; a return to values, as in "the good old days", to be precise.

Great. That's it; perhaps the revolution we need today is this: a step back to recover a few of the basic elements that we risk losing now because we're so busy looking ahead.

The first "basic element" is understanding why we devise advertising campaigns for our clients; that is to say, why we help them achieve commercial success (which explains why the British use the term TVCs – TV Commercials).

We discussed this extensively in the first chapter and inevitably we shall return to it later on.

Another key point to bear in mind is that the aim of any form of communication (and I emphasize “any”, so advertising is no exception) is to get a message across from A to B. This is what we learn on any basic course, even a correspondence course. In technical terms, manuals refer to transmitters (A) and receivers (B). In advertising we speak of brands (A) and target audiences (B). No offence to the Well-Intentioned Innovator-Integralist described earlier, and of all those who will take offence at hearing themselves referred to as targets.

What unites these two subjects is, of course, the message. The message, therefore, is the central element, the very essence of all communication. I know, I know, I’m saying it as though I were talking to an eight-year-old. I know: all you dear, evolved readers feel that I am stating the obvious. And yet I insist that I’m not stating the obvious: it is simple, yes, but certainly not a foregone conclusion; otherwise we targets would not be subjected daily to advertising campaigns wholly devoid of a brand message.

However, before we begin wading through the kinds of TV commercials to be shown in recent months, let us jaunt back to the fascinating past to retrieve a few classic examples of the centrality of the message in advertising. I’ve already cited Hopkins as one of my heroes. In this instance too, he comes to my aid. When faced with a brief, before getting his right hemisphere into gear to seek outstanding creative solutions, he first engaged his left one, petitioning rationalism to help him understand the right content for getting his message across.

Then came the study; the in-depth investigation and understanding of the product with a view to discovering its distinguishing feature. This is the same element that Rosser Reeves went on to define as the USP (Unique Selling Proposition). One good example of Hopkins' approach was his study of a campaign for a brand of beer. He was struck by the discovery that all the glass beer bottles were sterilized before being filled and capped. All this is standard procedure in the brewing industry, but a fact not widely known in the consumer world. So, his left hemisphere suggested to the creative Hopkins that this would be the right message: the target would have interpreted it as a guarantee of the quality and purity of the beer being advertised. The beer in question was Schlitz Beer, at the time just one of the many brands in the US, and it shot to being the number one beer on the market (before Hopkins came along, it was in eighth place!).

Skimming through my sources (both printed and digital), I haven't come across the advertisement in question to be able to tell you about its creativity. But that's almost better: here the idea is the message itself. Once you have the right message, the campaign is (almost) complete.

And so on to the present day. Let's think of the

big spenders in advertising. In Italy, among the top investors are the telephone companies. Italian footballer Francesco Totti and his wife Ilary versus actor Christian De Sica, and TV celebrity Belen (and now Neri Marcoré & Co) versus comedians Aldo, Giovanni and Giacomo. Three of the top-spending companies in terms of advertising budget who say absolutely nothing with their advertisements. Or do I err?

I do not wish to appear superficial: I'm well aware that the main driving factor when choosing a telephone company is the price, and that the message that the TIM, Vodafone, Wind and Tre commercials have to get across is a tactical one that changes over time. However, this, in my opinion, does not justify the complete absence of a brand message. With all their economic resources, are these institutes really incapable of coming up with anything better? No, impossible; I'm not buying it.

I think we've entered a vicious circle in which the brands are engaged in warfare (and not just attacking with free SMS messages and unlimited internet access) involving the deployment of endorser bombs and GRP. It's rather as if all the competitors were saying: "buy my brand". If Hopkins were here, or the legendary Bernbach, would they agree to writing witty sketches for TV comedians? Again: I don't think so.

What did Avis have to say that was so different from Hertz? Nothing, of course. And yet Bernbach created the famous "Numbertwoism campaign" and coined the phrase "We Try Harder", which to this day still appears beneath the red and white logo of the giant car rental firm. And what could Hertz say at that point? It pondered over it a while, then along came a certain Jim Durfee who wrote such an obvious statement that it went down in history. This is how it ran, more or less: "For years Avis has been telling you that we are number one. Now we'll tell you why." This paved the way for reams of body copy.

Far be it from me (self-styled advertising innovator) to think that the time has passed; to illude myself that an advertisement like Avis's would enjoy the same success today. Media, language, society, people ... everything has since changed. And I'm no nostalgic for yesteryear. On the contrary, I agree with those who say that this is the most exciting period in history for advertising.

For all this, I repeat: new advertising has to find its most contemporary form (and I'm convinced that adding a couple of elements to the creative duo is a sound formula, otherwise I wouldn't have written this book), but it has to retrieve some main ingredients from grandma's recipe book: healthy staples. A clear-cut, interesting, simple message is the foundation of everything.

Without the right message, advertising is just pure image, a question of more or less brilliant execution. It may even get itself noticed and be remembered. However, it is hardly likely to work. And if I'm told "TIM and Vodafone still sell", I reply, with no fear of contradiction, that it is only due to the pressure of advertising, not to creativity. Sure, they could (perhaps) lose points if they got their campaigns completely wrong. However, they'd still sell, whether they engaged the services of the best director or got their endorsers to write their own scripts. What are advertisers for?

Ah, I'd love to be able to dine with the CEO of one of these giants and throw down the gauntlet. It could be done. In spite of the crowds, mêlée and background noise, I'm sure that there would still be scope for a good message (a well-communicated one) to make all the difference. Perhaps one that stems from a product innovation studied by agency and client together (we'll come back to this point!). And maybe in ten years' time we'll read in advertising books how, thanks to some advertising foresight or other, TLC's company "Xyz" (the one who will answer my petition) brushed off its competitors.

I know, I'm dealing in fantasy-advertising here, but let us at least allow ourselves a little romanticism in this book. (Incidentally, car manufacturers are churning out the same advertising campaigns almost all over the world. Someone has even conducted a scientific experiment to demonstrate the fact. However, as always, there are exceptions and there have been some outstanding and memorable campaigns, particularly with press ads and billboards, where it's often hard to see more than just a three-quarter packshot and a financing offer.)

My final ingredient for a return to the basics is as obvious as the previous two but, if possible, even more overlooked: an advertising campaign should add value to the brand and/or brand product. Before you laugh at this umpteenth platitude, try thinking of the best commercials you've seen recently. You'll find that some of them are unequivocally associated with the brand (many of the Heineken ads can only be associated with Heineken). Others could belong to any brand and sometimes even any product.

If you readers out there are truly observant (an occupational defect, I should imagine) and you associate each campaign with the right product, try experimenting with your five-a-side team-mates or with the friends you go on holiday with. You'll say I'm right: remember the one with the dancing walrus? Yes, it's for chewing gum (but can we be sure? And if so, which one?). And the one with the squirrel that raises its tail and ... now, that was funny ... but was that for chewing gum as well? Maybe, but if so, which brand? And then there's the one about the boy whose breath freezes the lake ... Ah no, that one was for toothpaste. Could this be because now the emphasis is less on concepts and more on entertainment?

Ed McCabe said in an interview (cited by Pia Elliot in Just Doing It, published by Lupetti): "Every single commercial is all show business: the emphasis is more on special effects than on concepts and I don't know how much of this stuff remains in people's minds."

To recapitulate, the moral is that advertising today will have to change a lot to be able to call itself truly new. It should not, however, forget certain basic principles in advertising. On the contrary, it should recover and relaunch them. Among these, the three most obvious ones are the ones I've mentioned up to now, and they stem directly from the nous of our grandparents. For emphasis I shall call them the three commandments of future advertising:

Advertising, past and present, aims to promote the sales of a given product.

The core of an advertising campaign is a clear and simple message aimed at a specific target that will be able to understand it and find it interesting.

Bearing its target in mind, an ad campaign should be unequivocally associated with the brand/product behind the campaign.

To these three commandments I shall add an interpretive note so that everything can be summed up in a single word: creativity. Let's not forget it.

Right, before leaving the past to look to the future, I'll just point out one more thing so as to fend off any objections: my first commandment is in no way meant to suggest that every campaign should achieve tactical results. Product sales may also be promoted in the long term by building a brand and its positioning with patience and farsightedness. However, the campaign should always contribute to achieving the marketing objectives (hence business objectives) of the client firm.

And this excludes campaigns designed on a superficial level just to lend visibility to an original idea, to win prestigious awards, to earn more money with one medium compared to another, to satisfy (although on a subconscious level) the whim of a client or creative, or more simply because due attention isn't paid to addressing the question: is this campaign the one I'd go for if I were the client, that is if I were the one paying for its production and the medium to increase my company's turnover?

So now let's move on. After having seen what's good in the old-fashioned sense of advertising, and rescuing it from the pitchforks of revolution, let's now explore what needs to be added to the basic ingredients for this evolution (which we all feel is needed) to take place.

PART II
MULTIPLICATION

5

THE TWO-PERSON AGENCY

If the chapter that inspired the title of this book was about a creative duo comprised of four elements (and soon we'll see how), then this chapter is about an agency – the one that produces the sought-after, yearned-for advertising of tomorrow – that cannot survive alone. It takes two. The two entities in question, both of which are dependent upon one another, are the agency (obviously) and the client.

We touched on this earlier when discussing mobile phone companies which could, perhaps, rise above the hoi polloi if they decided to work shoulder to shoulder with an advertising agency. Not merely through creative briefing and asking that all production and coordination efforts be very closely linked to the crucial time-to-market theme, competition and battle of offers, but also by involving the advertising agency in the overview of the business, taking time together to think hard and hit on the right message and the right idea, as well as being willing to question elements of the product on offer.

To make myself clearer, once again I shall refer to a famous episode in the history of advertising in which the protagonist, this time a woman, is one Mary Wells. We're back in the sixties and Wells has been hired by Braniff Airlines, a US airline, to study an advertising campaign. In those days there were lots of airline companies and they were all very similar in terms of service and offer. It was hard to find a powerful message, a quality or a distinguishing element simply by skimming Braniff's characteristics.

Then came the flash of intuition: before communicating the uniqueness of the company, let's make the company unique. All the competitors' aircraft featured silver-grey fuselages (or at most they had a few more lines for chromatic identity). So why don't we (we = client + agency) create a *multicolour company*? Let's paint the planes, let's create a lively interior environment, let's give the air-hostess uniforms a fancy style. Braniff was able to communicate what it was that made it the airline of choice using a claim based on a simple pun: *The End of the Plain Plane.* This launched what Mark Tungate (author of the preface of this book, but more importantly of the wonderful *Adland – A Global History of Advertising)* described as "the world's most glamorous and sexy sixties airline".

Without complicity between client and agency, we would not have witnessed the success of this campaign or the company. This type of collaborative relationship was a winning element in the past, as it is in the present. In the future, however, given that this is the field we intend to explore, it will be even more so. And here ("at last", I hear you say) I stop looking in the rear-view mirror and look ahead, towards the changes in positions and attitudes of latter-day consumers.

What do consumers (new or old) have to do with the client-agency relationship? Loads. For new consumers – as my revolutionary friends emphasize, and this time I'm not being ironic – have changed. They are much more aware, knowledgeable, interested and attentive. Moreover, they have access to far more means (internet, first and foremost) for understanding, investigating, verifying and comparing notes with one another on a given product or brand.

So brands cannot tell a pack of lies anymore. They may not necessarily have done so to date, but they certainly had greater room for manoeuvre in the past. Nowadays, when advertisers make a claim, they know that people will check it out – maybe not everyone, but several will. And if the claim turns out to be false, there may be grave consequences: he who lies once, even over something trivial, or even in good faith, is a liar; and one cannot trust a liar. So, thanks to a simple syllogism, one cannot trust that brand and, therefore, one cannot purchase it.

If we reverse this point of view and make it positive, we return to dear old Bernbach who claimed that there was no better means of communication than a satisfied customer.

So this is how important it is, in the present and future scenario, that producer and advertiser engage in intense dialogue. The advertiser has to conduct an in-depth study to identify the opportunities that the brand has to offer in terms of communication. The company has to listen to the advertiser who advises for or against a certain message, or a certain tone or a certain attitude. Communication and product must say the same thing. I'll exaggerate (but I'm convinced that I'm not exaggerating): communication and product must be the same thing.

A perfect example of this concept comes from Crispin Porter + Bogusky, Burger King's agency. Copywriter Rob Reilly was working on a campaign when he came up with the idea of Chicken Fries: the same shape as fries, but made from chicken. Since their launch in 2004 they have been one of the chain's best-selling product innovations. And Bogusky claims (figures to hand) that that idea contributed to the success of Burger King more than any other multi-award-winning campaign.

A few years back, when I sat at international DDB meetings, the term co-create was already being bandied about. A team of world planners worked for months, years perhaps, on a new tool that envisaged four-person work phases between client and agency. And in any case, the legendary DDB tool called Brand Foundation was (and is) an excellent system for brand analysis using in-depth interviews and mind games with corporate management figures within companies.

However, this is something completely different – here we're talking about another step forward, towards the veritable coincidence of the roles. The agency has to get involved in the client's business, throwing itself wholly into it. It must see the purchase of one more packet of Nescafé as a success to be celebrated. At my agency, when we're deciding which team (account planners, creatives etc) is to look after a new client, I often say: the right one is the one in love with the product and most naturally suited to both it and its brand. So the agency has to be a bit like the client. It should get mad if the Tra Galbusera savoury biscuits, a brand whose campaign it created, are not on supermarket shelves.

Likewise, the client must also be a bit like the agency. It should contribute constructively without closing any doors beforehand and without getting inexperienced youngsters with no decision-making powers whatsoever to handle all the phases of an ad campaign. For if the agency were to say: "Let's make chicken fries", in the absence of someone with decision-making powers, the idea would be binned ... and any business opportunities for the client along with it. No newly hired employee should have to take the trouble to research an idea with so many implications and hence complications. We are all human.

Most recently, I happened to be chatting to one of my

clients who, acknowledging the potential of four-person intervention to create a great campaign, agreed to follow me in this direction. Unfortunately to date (December 2011), work is still in progress and so I cannot reveal the details. It is of little importance, however, because the story is true and still comprehensible even without naming names. As we were saying: agency and company, their sleeves rolled up, share the same aim – that of finding out how creativity can generate success in terms of the sale of the product advertised. We discussed the product in question at length as well as current and potential targets. With very little research material to hand and, moreover, years of stagnation in sales growth trends, we agreed that identifying the target would also be a creative job. So we arranged to work together, company and agency, around the same table.

All fine, up to this point, but then things began to creak. I said something like "perhaps an idea will come to us that will make package modification necessary" and my client told me quite calmly not to worry: he had already instructed an agency specialized in packaging to revise it. "They're really good, you know, Emanuele; they're the ones who recently redesigned the -beep- and -beep- packagings."

Oh no, that's not how it's supposed to work! Of course I knew how good the people at that agency are. Of course I knew that package design requires the ad hoc skills of specialists, and of course I knew that our kaleidoscopic agency does not have an in-house team with such a degree of experience and expertise in this field. But that wasn't the point. The point was that it is wrong to instruct a design agency (however great) without having first identified the core idea. And what if, unexpectedly and thanks to a great piece of intuition, we suddenly decided that the ideal target for our product was not the purchasers, but children? Perhaps a more playful packaging would be required, right? What if we decided to sell the product on the claim that it was easier to open because the limitation of all rival products is their ease of use? We'd have to study packaging that lived up to its promise, obviously.

I'm going to quote the past again: I don't think either Mary Wells (or her agency) were the ones to repaint the entire Braniff Airlines fleet, but the idea of doing it stemmed from the same idea for how to relaunch the company. And so, dear client, wait before passing on a creative brief to the brand design agency. Perhaps we might be able to do it together after having found our communication key.

Fortunately, we were in time and, more importantly, we agreed. So, for the time being, all package redesign is suspended. The legendary 'beep' agency (they really are good) will get to work on it as soon as we are ready to discuss the aim with them. And this will not be (as it was until recently) just a matter of revamping and "reviving" the historic product.

Work is still in progress as I write this book. Who knows;

perhaps a case history similar to that of Absolut vodka will come about. Or, as is more likely, a great job will come of it, a job as it should be done, that will make its important contribution to increasing the sales of the product.

Here's another story (I'm in anecdotal vein here). This story doesn't involve me directly, but it is very interesting for supporting the theory of this chapter: that the alliance between agency and client and the coalition between communication and product are now more than ever a must in the current socio-economical scene.

The protagonist in this story is Hyundai, which a few years ago, in 2008, achieved extraordinary success in the US thanks to an advertising campaign that did not focus on the car itself, but on a service instead. I don't know the details of how things developed between client and agency, but it all probably went something like this. Hyundai wrote a creative brief asking the agency to handle a particularly challenging objective: selling cars during one of the most acute phases of the worst economic crisis of the last thirty years. There was talk of recession on TV and American car giants in Detroit were desperately trying to avoid bankruptcy.

Fortunately, the cavalry stepped in (for once the heroes are the advertisers, hooray!) to lend Hyundai a hand. And what a hand. The reasoning was simple and linear, as is always the case with a successful plan (to quote John Hannibal Smith). If people weren't buying cars, it wasn't just because they couldn't afford one at the time. The crisis wasn't just an "economic" issue; it was, first and foremost, about trust. People were scared and the news reports weren't doing anything to assuage their fears (on the contrary). So the solution was to reassure consumers with an attempt to eliminate the financial risk associated with the purchase of a new car.

Great idea, but how? Agency and client sat down together around the decision table to find a way of turning the idea into an extraordinary success. This is how the Hyundai Assurance Plus plan came into being. It told American consumers: buy your car from us and, should you be unlucky enough to lose your job during the first year, you can return it to us and we'll take it back without any expenditure on your part. The result of the campaign, as broadcast by BBC news, was as follows: in the month during which Chrysler lost 55%, General Motors 49% and Ford 40%, Hyundai, "thanks to a new advertising campaign" (as the TV commentator said – you can hear it on YouTube) was the only car company in countertrend. That month it chalked up a +14% increase on the previous year. The campaign won awards, Hyundai got its breath back and the rest of the market followed suit.

And again the question (now rhetorical) comes round: would a similar case history have been possible had the agency remained shut up inside its office, focusing on how to talk about the solidity and reliability of Korean cars?

If the agency hadn't been able to go to the client and say: "we've had an idea, want to try it?", nothing would have happened. I don't think an advertising agency has the skill for the financial study of a product-service project like Assurance Plus: external company involvement would have been necessary, so there must have been an investment in internal resources to collaborate closely and so "clinch" the idea of an advertising campaign. Singlehandedly the agency would not have got anywhere. This is why I am hammering on about this concept and, I repeat: now, more than ever, the agency is a twosome.

I haven't the faintest idea about who will read this book. I don't know if most of you will be those in the trade (hence colleagues), or academics, or students (some of whom will be forced to read it because I'll be including it in my course reading lists!), or company men, or readers who simply find the topic interesting. Whatever the case, after completing the theoretical arguments of this chapter in the hope that I have convinced my readership of the necessity of a partnership between us (advertisers) and them (clients), I hereby dedicate these last heartfelt lines exclusively to them (the clients). The author hereby grants other members of the reading public to skip directly to the next chapter.

As for you, my dear agency clients, please bear with me for a few paragraphs longer. If you have found anything that makes sense in this chapter then accept part of the responsibility (50%, in fact), because what happens on a daily basis does not correspond with the aforementioned cases. And you do your best to ensure that what you deem right in theory is then continued in the project.

In the meantime I'll use my pen-and-paper pulpit to take the liberty of asking you to reflect on two aspects in particular: the involvement of your communication partner and their relative remuneration.

Let's begin with the first of these: how to hire the right agency. The most common way, at least in Italy, of choosing an advertising partner is by means of a competition and, personally, I can't see anything wrong with that. On the contrary. Not being an avid aficionado of the Milanese aperitif, it's handy when a major company decides to make several agencies compete instead of relying directly on personal acquaintances. However, aside from my biased interest, I think that getting several agencies to work on the same creative brief is a good way of getting to know them, and is more effective than just chatting in front of a glass of Ruinart (not that there's anything wrong with Ruinart, or with chatting, come to think of it). Of course, competitions of this nature have to be well organized, their regulations and criteria clearly set out, and the client must be able to truly compare the approach and strategy-creative skills of the participating agencies.

Here is an important point then, that fits into my logic of the matter: in my opinion, the client should choose the agency, not the campaign. I'll even say this, dear readers: if, one day, I were to end up working for you (never say never) and had to choose an agency with which to collaborate, I would devise an ad hoc creative brief, one probably wholly unconnected with the objective of that moment, in order to assess the agency's potential under various aspects: its thought strategy, its creative potential, its skill in execution, its complete neutrality in relation to the media and its expertise in different fields and media.

Then there is always the fact that what is presented during a competition seldom becomes the advertising campaign produced. It is quite obvious: it is virtually impossible for an agency, basing itself solely on information received during the creative brief phase and without dialogue with the company, to create a perfect campaign. However, aside from all this, I return to the purport of the question: if all that we said earlier about the enormous potential of teamwork is true, it is obvious that the aim of selection is to identify the right partner with which to build successful campaigns over time.

It's the same with women (or men, depending on your sexual inclination): if I want a good time, I'll probably go for the prettiest girl (if I can choose); the one I find most physically attractive. Or maybe even the bubbliest, most imaginative one. However, if I am to choose my lifetime partner I might think about it more and weigh up other factors as well. Intellectual affinity becomes the fundamental requisite (while it doesn't come into the equation at all for a night of passion). Her view of the world would matter to me. Then there's reliability, the sharing of aims and undertakings. Sure, I have to like her, and a lot too. You cannot plan and choose the woman of your life based on rational schemes without being in love with her. If the intention is to travel along a road together, mutual understanding is imperative and you have to know that you are more or less following the same route.

Let's go beyond the metaphor: an agency for a one-shot project can be chosen according to the idea presented. However, the advertising agency on which to base major goals cannot and must not be regarded as a one-shot agency. And clients too, who by the nature of their business or budget limit always find themselves working on individual projects, would do well to ask themselves: if these different projects have a single director, would this not perhaps reflect positively on the results, not only in terms of efficiency (constant agency-changing is an extremely time-consuming affair for all concerned) but in terms of brand communication?

A fixation of mine is the idea that lots of tactical actions placed in a row and looked at at the same time should result in a single image: the combination of their voices should be able to reflect something unique and distinctive about the brand whose name they bear.

Therefore, dear readers, here is my heartfelt piece of

advice: once you have identified an agency that seems to have the right characteristics and chemistry to be your agency, do not propose contracts that are overly short term. If you want to protect yourselves, include a nice little unilateral rescission clause so you can fire them whenever you want to. In 1970, divorce entered the Italian legal system because it suddenly became clear that the eternal state of a relationship, however desirable, could not be imposed by law or contract. Allow yourselves the possibility of being able to leave your agency whenever you are tired of it, but begin with a pledge in good faith that sanctions your intention: I, client, take you, agency, to be my partner with which to go far. To build together. Without an expiry date around the corner.

Once again, as I pen these lines, I feel as though I'm stating the obvious. And yet it's not so obvious if it's true – and how true it is – that in many countries the prevailing trend among companies is that of splitting budgets into projects which are assigned on an individual basis each time to the agency that delivers the most interesting idea on the lowest budget.

And it's the use of the word "budget" that brings me to the second aspect of collaboration that I wish to draw to the attention of my client readers: the remuneration of agencies. However, please believe me when I say that I'm not doing this with a view to basking in this moment of glory as you read my book to feather my own nest. I do so to add another theoretical element to the main theory of this book. A theory that I summarize thus: advertising remains one of the most extraordinary tools on the market for achieving commercial success, but it must evolve into more modern and suitable models, which we shall attempt to describe here.

I envisage these new models changing several of the standard models, such as the idea that creativity is a trade open solely to art directors and copywriters, or that the strategic planning of agencies must be handled by traditional brand planners. However, besides that which agencies can and should do in order to change, the involvement of other players in communication is necessary: on the one hand the consumers (and we shall see how I believe they may be included in the process), and on the other the user companies. And this quickly leads us to the subject of money. Money, as we know, is something that makes everything prosaic. Yet money is the fuel of good work.

While I detest waste – I hate it when I see agencies today still trying to convince clients that the light in the Caribbean is something else, so if they want a photograph to turn out well ... Yet at the same time I see how a lot of the quashing of creative quality (the kind that leads to results for companies, but not to awards for art directors) is sadly attributable to the difficulty that agencies have in seeing their contribution to ideas and strategies duly appreciated.

If, in order to survive (economically), a creative team is obliged to work on ten clients at a time, how can it possibly have the physical time and mental capacity to create the campaign of the century?

Moreover, on the subject of economic paradox, as I stated in the preface, today advertising is harder, more complex and involves more figures and professions. And yet less is being paid for it. I think something is amiss. Either someone is missing out, or everyone is missing out.

However, enough on the subject of vile money.

Let's turn the page to another chapter to return to our starting point, and see what this book offers on new ways of devising advertising campaigns.

6

THE PLANNER TRINITY

I'll get straight to the point: today the traditional "Planner", as we know him, just cannot hack it singlehandedly. But this isn't because the objective of his role is different to what it was back in the sixties, at the time when this figure was gradually introduced into all major advertising agencies.

The aim of the game remains the same: study, analysis, understanding the brand and the consumers, identifying opportunities and having insight; showing a strategic path along which the creative team can potter and explore and come up with all sorts of ideas, but with a clear objective in mind: to get the right message across by writing the creative brief and supporting the creative team along the way to prevent dangerous straying. The profession remains the same; it's just that today things are more complex.

The necessary skills and, moreover, the mental make-up required for writing a creative brief in the modern era (as outlined by different players ranging from the "Post-Digital Age" to the "Consumer Control Era") are diverse.

This is why I say that today the Planner cannot possibly be a single person. It is likely that the evolution of the species already has DNA in the pipeline for a new kind of Planner with all the necessary requisites. Or perhaps there already is one somewhere in the world. Nevertheless, even if one does exist, he/she will need be a trinity – that referred to in the title of this chapter. This trinity, in my view, is essential to the creation of advertising today. And of tomorrow.

The first musketeer in this trinity is, without doubt, the traditional account planner (the brainchild of Stanley Pollitt), aka the *brand planner* or *strategic planner*. The official birth of this figure dates back to the sixties, so its relative skills have been consolidated by years of history. It is covered by precise job descriptions, work methods and tools, and there are also teachers, books, case histories and market parameters for it. And as always, of course, there are also many ways of interpreting the role, however codified. So some "traditional" planners are more sociologists and anthropologists, others more researchers and data analysts, others still more psychologists. Others investigate the truth like philosophers (allow me to say what a boon it would be for planners to study philosophy!). Others build up theories, arguments and presentations like lawyers. Yet the discipline of the account planner is singular: refining the brand-consumer relationship. Insight. The message. Anything that correlates the two communication entities within the right context.

The second element of the strategy trinity is what I call the *digital strategist*. There aren't many handbooks to help us with the job description of this one. Surfing the net or reading a few recent publications (particularly in English) will provide several definitions, but there is no "correct" one defined by the Oxford English Dictionary equivalent to the term used in the world of advertising. So I'll give you my own personal description, so that we understand one another.

The digital strategist is the "digital fluent" version of the planner. He studies consumer behaviour (just like the classic planner) but his main sources for this are usually social media, blogs and the web. He relies on *conversation analysis* as opposed to market research, and instead of studying focus groups he listens to people through *crowdsourcing*.

He investigates the trends (just like your classic planner) but does so by analysing the most searched words on search engines, the most viewed videos, those most shared on YouTube, the posts most commented on and the most popular app downloads. His guiding light is not Eurisko, but Google Trends.

He studies competitors and the competition (just like your classic planner) but does so while bearing in mind which key words are controlled by the various brands, what type of engagement online brands propose, and which values are effectively attributed by people to companies and products (beside the payoffs that brands use to describe their positioning).

It is the task of the digital strategist to move from observer to analyst to identifier of opportunities. Which free spaces? Which themes should be controlled? What are the target's needs? In short, exactly what the classic planner does, but using different tools and a different mental make-up. If it is true, as Teressa Iezzi writes in her book *Idea Writers*, that "digital is not a channel, digital is how you live your life", then the digital strategist represents the knowledgeable authority on a new way of experiencing the world, regardless of medium, be it digital or physical.

There are on-the-ground campaigns which, semantically speaking, are 100% digital. One example for all of them: the Fun Theory, DDB Sweden's idea for Volkswagen that was subsequently adapted for other countries. In all its variations passers-by are "induced" to behave in an eco-friendly manner, for which their reward, quite simply, is fun. So, if someone preferred to exit the Stockholm underground using the healthy option of climbing the stairs as opposed to riding the polluting escalator, his reward was that the stairs rang out – each step had been turned into a giant piano key and corresponded to a musical note. What is so different about asking people to pass on one side instead of another from asking them to click on one link instead of another?

I have no idea which professional figures were involved in Stockholm, but I was lucky enough to have worked for Volkswagen and so helped to create the Italian version of Fun Theory. As such I am well aware of who contributed to the conception of our idea. Well: the team (inevitably) included people blessed with a good head and digital fluency.

It was thanks also to their input that we developed Blue Christmas in Milan. It was an international success story. Here it is. We installed an "instant plastic bottle and cardboard recycling machine" in the city. People were invited not to waste recyclable materials. The reward for those who used the magic contraption was to receive a Christmas decoration recycled from the crushed object they had introduced into the machine only moments earlier. Along with the decoration there was a tag featuring the name of the initiative and some eco-friendly advice for a waste-free Christmas.

So, if digital is not just digital (as my friend and partner Stefano Pagani is fond of saying), then the digital strategist must bring to the planning room not only his knowledge of technological tools but also a profound knowledge of new languages and hence of the new world.

And the third element of the trinity?

Here it is. Let's call this figure the *Business Planner*, even though (as we shall discover shortly) this moniker is not necessarily a new one. A premise is necessary here, as briefly mentioned earlier on the subject of the agency-client relationship, and even before that when highlighting the correlation between the success of an advertising campaign and the results of a client's business. This has always been true, as it was in the instance of Braniff in the sixties, and as it is now with Hyundai in recent years (to stick to examples already examined). However, aside from general recommendations, what are the practical implications?

Well, the creative team has to remember that its task is to be "truly motivated to sell and to make a difference to its client's business" (to quote Teressa Iezzi again). Fair enough. But is this so easy? Not always. Sometimes the agency's task is to enhance the ideas and products of its clients as much as possible with a first-rate campaign. But at other times it is possible (if not necessary) to do more. The challenge today, so everyone says, is to seek business solutions. Strawberry Frog, currently one of the finest agencies around, states its mission on its website. Between the lines, its corporate objective is visible: to devise "solutions that generate growth for our clients" using strategy and creativity.

If the agency truly wishes to find business solutions,

then it must familiarize itself with the business. Someone has to be capable of analysing it in-depth, reading the figures and understanding the logic behind production and distribution. They have to be able to imagine where new margins can be carved. They must, for all intents and purposes, represent the client's viewpoint at the agency. As we have said, knowledge of the market in which the client is moving is essential ... but that alone is not enough. They must also be familiar with the plans of the company that the agency works for. They must go there regularly and experience it on a day-to-day basis and communicate with it.

Marketing skills, business acumen, visiting companies, communicating with the clients ... Don't you feel that there are many similarities between the job description of this business planner and that of the account manager? You should, unless you happen to be among those who hold the profession of the account manager to be on a par with that of a lackey or a red-tapist, or an organizing secretary. Personally, I see many similarities. Doing so can save agencies the bother of having to employ a new figure especially. They would have what they need within the firm already, if needed. So for once, it's about drawing up a new work model and not creating new professional figures from scratch. It won't be such a simple task when it comes to the creative team, but I feel rather confident on the planning front.

Sure, according to this logic, when selecting the account planners one has to be able to identify those who understand (and are interested) in marketing – real marketing, that is, the kind studied in the faculty of economics, not at communication schools. One should have a preference for people blessed with innate business acumen. How many times have you heard or uttered the words *return on investment*? The account planner (the one who turns *business planner* when necessary) is the figure within an agency who, better than others, knows how to go beyond the demagogic value of this expression. And I'll repeat this at the risk of wearing both you and myself out: it isn't just a question of skills, it's a mental attitude.

(I'd like to open a small parenthesis. On the subject of the account manager, a figure that is often erroneously underrated is Tom Carrol, the CEO at TBWA, whose opinion is interesting: "Good creative people always saw the value in strong account people, weak creatives never did." However, besides strong creatives, you also need strong account people, of course.)

That's it then. This is my recipe for today's kind of planning. Three heads that together brainstorm, rub off, put up with and inspire one another with the aim (let's not forget it) of synthesizing their work into a concise, yet inspiring, creative brief – for the creative brief (it's tautological) should be concise.

"I like a simple brief: one page" says Evan Fry, one of

the founders of Victors & Spoil. The creative brief should be the conclusion that brilliant trained minds reach after having examined a situation from all possible angles. Studying, pondering and processing. The creative brief ought to be an indication of the direction to be taken, of the message to be conveyed.

What is it that we wish to remain in the minds of those who see our campaign? The creative brief is that sheet of paper that the creative team should keep pinned to the cork pinboard near their desk for the entire duration of the creative phase. They should get up from time to time to go to the planner trinity and ask for more information or clarification on a point. Or even simply to compare notes or for a shoulder to cry on. One great planner, Henrick Habberstad, defined the art of planning as "the creativity behind the creativity", and the idea that the creative brief is a crucial step in the creative phase is something I agree with entirely.

If the brief is brief, then the briefing (i.e. the meeting during which the brief is presented and discussed with the creative team) should, on the other hand, have its due amount of time. The creative team needs to understand fully all the reasons behind the synthesis. It is always more profitable to doubt and discuss than to simply take things as gospel. At briefing meetings I have often witnessed intuition flourish into the creative concept of the campaign. There are also those who would like the art director and copywriter (and others that we shall see) to study all their cards because sometimes, in the meanders of information available, there lies the spark that will ignite the idea.

Rick Condos, for example (one of the creative directors behind Coca Cola's *Happiness Factory* campaign), says that the more information you can get, the more you are able to work together with the people who know the business, and the freer you feel in your creativity. However, not all people are like him. Usually there is no time to delve into clients' files, and the job of the planners is precisely that – of bringing the precious contribution of synthesis. They obviously do so not simply by summarizing the available information, but by interpreting and integrating it, creating logical shortcuts, coming to conclusions and arriving at insights, concepts and messages.

Were it up to me to decide (and were it possible in practical and economic terms), I'd like the planner's work output to be double all the time. On the one hand, a one-page brief; on the other, an entire book on the brand and the product, with lots of anecdotes, intriguing stories and interviews with managers and consumers. This would be anything between eighty and one hundred well-bound pages that the creative team could keep on their bedside table and read before turning out the light at night or over the weekend. Obviously, the book I have in mind would have to be penned by three people. Maybe one day I will write it: I'll set up the "Flying Cow" publishing house specializing in in-depth fictional advertising briefs. They'd be short-lived, but they'd be a great hit with the clients (everyone enjoys reading about themselves) and the creatives at Condos. If only. For now I'll just settle for a *brief brief* and a *long briefing*.

Before turning the page (both figuratively and literally), here is a brief summary and a final circumstantiation.

In my view, the modern planner has three heads: that of the *brand planner*, that of the *digital strategist* and that of the *business planner* (hidden inside an account manager). I've already stated that perhaps somewhere in the world there already is someone who embodies these three sides of my "superbeing", but I've had no wind of them to date. I have, however, in my professional life, encountered people whose working and reasoning methods encapsulate the characteristics of all three. There are planners from the world of CRM, for example, who have an uncanny knack for understanding the droll logic of marketing (and of the economy), combined with an outstanding sociological sensitivity. Planners from web agencies, and as such perfectly fluent digitally speaking, are very good at discussing marketing and research data. There are account managers with a huge vocational strategy.

This means that, notwithstanding what I'm about to state most assertively in the following chapter, sometimes compromises to the trinity can be found. And one day, when culture permits, when schools start training youngsters for the professions of today and tomorrow and not for those of yesteryear, the brand planner who speaks a digital language and talks about distribution and marginalities will be born. And he shall be known as The Planner. To paraphrase Mary Wells, it would be nice to witness "the birth of the plain planner".

7

THE CREATIVE DUO IS A FOURSOME. PLUS ONE.

At last, the big moment has come ... the chapter that made this book worth writing (and reading as well, if it was the number four that won you over).

I'm not the only one who says that the creative duo is no longer enough. You can see it everywhere – in books by advertising theorists and in declarations by international gurus of the profession. Sometimes you can even see it in the comments of our managers and creative directors. Many times in her recent book Teressa Iezzi quotes Benjamin Palmer, the outstanding creative person at Crispin Porter + Bogusky, who repeatedly emphasizes how the art director and copywriter duo is no longer enough. He even goes so far as to say: "We won't get very far in this day and age with that team [copywriter and art director]". In actual fact, Palmer talks of an extended team that embraces other specialists which, each time, support traditional creatives. Others, in describing the evolutions necessary for modernizing advertising agencies, talk more generally of greater teamwork between the various departments.

I have been preaching for years about the breaking down of barriers, the crossfire sharing of different experiences and visions, and the appreciation of ideas, whatever their origin (if you don't trust me then read my book, *Not Available* (2007), currently available only in Italian).

However, it's not 2007 anymore. The years have passed and I feel that the time has come, after a decent settling down and observation period, to acknowledge that the world really has changed and to propose new solutions that fit into this scenario, by imagining models that can stand the test of time while remaining open to evolution. If there is one thing that we have understood about this new era it is that speed is its basic element. We have not witnessed a sudden burst of acceleration that will simply lead us to a new place. We have realized that from now on we will no longer be standing at the station, but shall continue to work as we look through the windows at the changing landscape. However, we now have sufficient elements to be able to know in which direction our train is bound and as many again to know how the carriage interiors should be designed.

The backdrop is what many will define as the *Post-Digital Age*: the age in which the logic brought about by the explosion of the digital world (and not just by the technology of the digital world) has forever changed rules, relationships, behaviour patterns, media, values and attitudes. Others refer to this same thing as the *Consumer Control Era*. The meaning does not change, but in this definition the focus of the observer is more on a particular subject: the consumer, who (thanks again to progress and digital culture) takes control, thus making the transition from passive to active.

I'll allow myself a slight digression here, promising myself yet again that I will soon return to the thread of my discussion and get around to discussing my new idea of the creative duo, which is no longer a duo.

Once again this digression concerns my deep-rooted diffidence towards absolutism and categorization. In the same literature on the aforementioned sociological and cultural change (which only a blind man could fail to see and a simpleton minimalize), one sometimes reads statements that, personally, I find deeply perplexing. We're talking about those phrases for effect that paint a world in which everyone writes a blog, or prefers to create online web series than sprawl across a sofa and turn on the TV, or in which people are more willing to trust an anonymous post on Facebook than an article published in a science magazine.

I don't think that this is the world today. And not just because Italy's poorer provinces don't have broadband connections and the average age of the population is higher than the norm. I'm certain this will change. It won't happen overnight, but it won't take centuries either. However, people will remain different from one another.

For years it has been possible for anyone to call Radio 24, leave a political comment and feel gratified that their voice and their opinion will be heard by thousands of radio listeners. And yet not everyone does this. Anyone can buy two or three different daily newspapers or read them online, but not everyone does. Anyone can check up on the information they receive through adverts, but not everyone does. Neither should it be taken for granted that having the opportunity to take an active part in communication will make everyone want to do so, even though it will be increasingly easy, standard practice and more natural in the new post-digital society.

In the previous chapter on the client-agency relationship I wrote that today, more than ever, it is important that brands communicate in a transparent manner because their targets are more evolved, knowledgeable and critical. However, if it is true that before believing that the latest Fiat or BMW model is the best in its category I will search for comments on the web (as I always have done, as well as discussing it at the bar and buying Quattroruote, Auto Oggi and Gente Motori car magazines), it is equally true that when I reach for a product at the toothpaste counter I'll continue to do so without reading up on it first; maybe opting for the one my mind associates with something that struck me (an ad campaign, for example – just think!). Then if, as I brush my teeth, I realize that my toothpaste doesn't taste as nice as another brand, I doubt I shall sit down and post an online review as I would, say, for a hotel or a restaurant.

I say this only to avoid drifts towards absolutism, not to deny the obvious or paint an anachronistic picture. I'm convinced that I am living in the *post-digital age* (you'll have realized that of the two definitions I prefer this one), and it is for this very reason that I believe a profound change is necessary in the way advertising is produced.

However, let us go back to the creative duo; "let's go back" being the operative expression, for in this instance too it's worth looking back before looking ahead. The birth of the creative duo as a core element of advertising campaigns may be attributed to Bill Bernbach and traced back to 1949. But what about before then? Who created advertising? And why did the simple idea of putting two people with complementary skills together in the same room represent (as it says in the history books) the birth of the creative revolution?

Let's start in order. If you flick through the advertising annuals you'll see that in the early 1900s there were two main types of advertising campaign: the one that relied on the persuasive efficacy of a text and the other that was more like a work of art than an advertisement. The former, of course, was created by *writers*, and the latter by visual artists, illustrators and painters. Not that copy-based campaigns didn't have a layout. It just wasn't the important element and in any case it came later. A good graphic artist would have created the layout according to the creative's idea. And vice versa. The art director (or the artist, to be more precise) would find an image capable of conveying what he had in mind and draw it. Then he would leave a small space to be filled with the missing information. The idea, however, was already there. Toulouse Lautrec was an art director, but he didn't work as part of a duo.

At a certain point, however, the individual creative was no longer enough; or rather, someone realized that the "singlehanded" formula had less potential than a new formation comprising two minds getting together and brainstorming. This is what spawned the creative revolution: not so much stating that two professional figures (with complementary skills essential to a world in which advertising was all in print) would one day continue to share an office, but the magic that the union of two different viewpoints and two different sensibilities would create. And this is how the *Creative Team* came into being.

This was (and is, in effect; at least until the time this book went to press) the formation assigned to create any type of campaign. More than sixty years have elapsed since that first (successful) experiment, and advertising has changed a lot. And I'm not just referring to the age we live in. In the days of Dane Dolye Bernbach most advertising appeared in printed form – dailies, magazines, posters and so on. Then along came the TV commercial and advertisers had to learn new art forms: copywriters became screenwriters and art directors developed a strong feel for cinema. There have been moments in the history of advertising and film-making in which boundaries have become blurred and broken down. Film directors such as Alan Parker, Ridley Scott and David Lynch started out as creatives in an advertising agency; at the same one, incidentally: the British agency Collett Dickenson & Pearce.

It is obvious that, as with any trade, even the professions of art director and copywriter have evolved over the years. Today's train drivers no longer rely on the same skills as their predecessors who ran steam trains. An F1 driver can no longer dream of an epic Grand Prix win steering with a spanner instead of a wheel, as Nuvolari once did.

However, my theory on the extended duo isn't just limited to the evolution of the *art director* and *copywriter* species (which is nevertheless pondered and studied in depth). It actually begins with the idea that the creative duo is not just a set comprising two elements; it becomes an autonomous entity, and it wishes to foster an evolution of that entity. Thus, while the figures of copywriter and art director adapt as individuals to refine their skills and update their mental make-up, the creative duo is enriched by a new element to improve the execution of their trade: that of creating memorable and effective advertising campaigns.

Before announcing the team line-up for the match in this new stadium (and in this new sport, as was the case with snowboarding), one final observation, which, in actual fact, is more of a question to which I have never really found a genuine and convincing answer. Here it is: how is it that creative giants have, over time, always been willing to learn new techniques and languages and move with the times to pursue their creativity, and yet when the internet arrived they retreated, allowing new professional figures to handle it instead? Why their refusal to see the web scene (and now all the digital stuff) as something that could offer them new opportunities? They did their best to ignore its potential for as long as possible, until in the end they were forced to pay for external skills, dipping into what, in the meantime, had become another world.

Honestly, I really haven't the foggiest idea and I can't even begin to fathom the possible reasons for this. In 1996 (sixteen years ago!) I was desperately seeking a copywriter and an art director who were enthusiastic about the idea of creating the world's best banner. They were definitely other times, but I saw the banner as the evolution (and not the poor man) of billboarding and press advertising. I said to all the creatives I met along my young entrepreneurial way: think how great it would be – a poster that can be animated and even clicked on to reveal a hidden piece of advertisement that is just a second away. It's certainly more complex than a static advertisement, but just think of the amount of creative potential in it.

Let's leave effectiveness aside for the moment and examine it from an exclusively expressive and creative point of view. It's a new "object" for which the rules still have to be invented. It is a potentially fantastic space for creating a *teaser* (creatives have always had a penchant for teasers: aren't they the ones who have always fought against clients' budgets that do not provide for necessary planning?). It is a great way to assess in real time the pull of a creative idea and to compare lots of ideas and see which one most captures the public's attention.

The curiosity of a creative person is (or at least should be) satisfied by knowing if his idea works or not. Often he has no way of knowing; he relies on awards from juries whose actions he doesn't always approve of or on the comments of those in the sector. And yet all these reasons are not enough. In my opinion, in those days no great creative was as enraptured as he should have been. Why was this?

There, I've said it now, but I don't have an answer. The certainty is that the consequences of this slothful creativity led to a medium that had the potential to change the world. (I say "potential" because I'm referring to 1996. Obviously what was potential then is now reality.) The main consequence was that the web agencies had control over the steering wheel and the web agencies – even the best ones – lacked the stature for this task. There are no creative duos in this kind of set-up. They don't have the right DNA; they don't reason by concept but by execution. Thus art direction morphed into web design and copywriting became editorial writing. Web agencies have always channelled their efforts and investments more into form than into substance and more into technique than into ideas. I don't know a single creative (or creative director) of an Italian web agency who holds a place in the Hall of Fame in the Art Directors' Club. And this is through no fault of the ADCI.

I recently went to the awards evening for one of Italy's most prestigious digital creativity awards and I came away a broken man. They said nothing. There was no inspiration, no emotion. All was dead calm with a few exceptions in the form of viral videos, and this probably simply because they had been "devised" (and not just made) by putting creativity first. Where, on the other hand, was the creative excellence in websites, competitions, banners, newsletters and special initiatives? There wasn't any, I can assure you. And is this because the digital environment isn't fertile ground for great ideas? I really don't think so.

Take a deeper look at the globe and you will find examples that tell an entirely different story. Most times however, and not only in Italy, we are still light years away. Is this the fault of the Italian web agencies that have never tried to stand out from the crowd using their ideas? Or is it the fault of "classic" creatives who remain on the outside looking in, losing interest in what's happening in the modern world? I'm not trying to pin the blame on anyone in particular, I'm just trying to paint a picture of how things are, which forms part of the backdrop for the definition of the concept of creativity (and identifying the means for developing it), and which should be a priority for everyone.

I've been speaking of the web, but the same thing applies to many other fields. You do know, don't you, that today most communication budgets are invested in sales promotions? And who invented them? Rarely have I heard the names of the most famous Executive Creative Directors associated with this type of activity. So zillions of posters wallpaper cities and speak of incredible price cuts and great competitions using exclamation marks galore, while true creatives spend their time on blogs complaining about the advertising world and its continuing demise.

On the other hand, the much-feted case history of David Droga for the New Zealand beer Steinlager is true promotional advertising. The same applies to direct marketing (because although it's true that mailing advertising to people's homes is expensive and often not very efficient, it is also true that talking to the right people on a one-to-one basis is one of the few keys that makes today's communication truly effective). And the same goes for events, which are often devised by wonderful producers or account planners who have never in their lives studied the basics of advertising.

So the backdrop is formed by this: the difficulty of agencies to systematically include non-advertising languages in ad campaigns, plus a lot more. This "a lot more", which I attempted to describe at the beginning of this book, is connected with social, cultural and moral change in our era, the proliferation of the media, overcrowding in advertising, the loss of efficacy of several means, and I'd say particularly the fact that advertising has lost its way – after having tried to defend conservative and reactionary stances, it has, in many instances, fallen into "the future at all costs" trap.

What does one do with such a backdrop? Each individual seeks his/her own answer, and if you've reached this page, now you will have mine: the way to broach the creation of an advertising campaign today is to leave the creative side to a team comprised of the following four figures: *Art Director, Idea Writer, Attention Planner* and *Digital Creative Planner.* Plus one more, who I'll call the *Creative Consumer*.

Before describing the individual players in this new team, here are two important pieces of advice for readers. The first one: remember at all times that the figures I describe in this chapter are to all effects creatives (noun, not adjective). The fact that they draw on other skills and mentalities classically associated with non-creatives (such as, for example, the media, PR or strategic planning) must not fool you in the analysis of my proposal.

What I am describing is not a flowchart to illustrate how the various departments can work together or a general underscoring of the fact that anyone can be creative (in the adjectival sense, not the nominal one). In this chapter we deal exclusively with the creative department, which until recently consisted of just an art director and a copywriter; now it is bolstered by interesting new figures that ideally work together as a team on a four-by-four basis, sharing duties, clients and briefs to create new-generation campaigns.

Here's the second piece of advice: don't make the mistake of thinking that this fantastic four only works when the client's (or the planner's) brief features words like digital, unconventional, events, viral videos, word-of-mouth etc. If I manage to explain the role of each member of this quartet then it will become obvious as to how this dream team would be the perfect modern answer, even for a TV campaign request with the *average housewife* as the target.

And so to work. It gives me great pleasure to present to you, in random order, the individual members of the new creative duo. As you will now be aware the duo is now a foursome, but be warned – it's a foursome ... plus one.

PART III

CREATIVES TODAY

8

THE ART DIRECTOR TODAY

Just so I don't seem too revolutionary, particularly in the wake of all my semantic distinctions, I shall begin my introductions with the only element of the creative team to retain his original job title, even though the content of his duties has changed slightly. Just as Italian is the official language in the world of music, so English is the language of marketing and communications. No-one has taken it upon themselves to translate the term *adagio* and, similarly, no-one in Italy has ever thought of finding an Italian equivalent of the names we use to describe the figures in the advertising world. *Art director* and *copywriter* remain the same in Italy as they do in almost all the rest of the world.

However, returning to the etymological meaning of "art director" helps me highlight the true role of this figure today. In the meantime, as I have done thus far and shall continue to do (and I hope our Latin forefathers were right when they said that repetition helps), again I ask you not to forget that first and foremost the task of the art director is to be a creative person; to come up with ideas regardless of his/her specific talent. Nowadays even a radio campaign is devised by a creative duo, and although it is typically the copywriter who drafts the script, it isn't a given that the idea, the mood or even the choice of voices cannot be subject matter for an art director.

That said, obviously the art director possesses a specific talent which he lays on for his team, and which is connected with his ability to handle the *art direction* of the project. In the past this field was certainly a lot easier to cover. If we think back to the very first press campaigns, it was often a question of executing the layout of a concept that had already been clearly expressed in words. Or conversely, it was about creating a powerful image that could convey the right message.

Think back to the wonderful posters of the early 1900s. At that time artistic direction and design coincided. Depero was an art director in the fullest sense of the term. Without being fully fledged art masters (and advertising history is full of these), in the past one could not have entertained the idea of becoming an art director without knowing how to draw, for the field was very much characterized by this figurative aspect – illustration, design, photography ... Marcello Dudovich, Armando Testa, Oliviero Toscani ...

all art directors of yesteryear. Not so very long ago, yet certainly in the past.

Then, of course, there were also films to contend with. As a youngster (let's say as a small boy), I used to love spending my afternoons at my uncle's advertising agency (it was called *Tonic*) where I would sit in silent fascination, watching the art directors as they prepared their storyboards using pencils, then Pantones (great colour felt-tips that you probably can't get any more – they would release a characteristic aroma of art and alcohol). There were no computers around (still, it was the eighties, not the Middle Ages). And yet everything was different. Nowadays it is common for an art director to be quite incapable of drawing a house with a tree next to it, and yet he might be a wizard with Photoshop or know how to create a video on a Mac that's virtually ready to broadcast.

So, what do Toulouse Lautrec, Armando Testa and a young art director of today, who is allergic to pencils and felt-tips, all have in common? I'd say *aesthetic sense* (as well as the ability to have ideas).

The essence of art direction, in my opinion, is having the skill to make what is shown attractive, be it a billboard or a TV commercial or – today – a website or an event. However, handling the aesthetic side does not just mean putting together all the elements in an organised, harmonious manner in an attempt to convey a pleasant image. It also entails making that image a vehicle for the message that is to be conveyed. And it is in this trickiest part that the talents of the best creatives come to the fore.

Creating an attractive image and filling that image with meaning: this is what an art director should know how to do. That said, the difference when compared to the past is cancelled out, don't you think? However, given that we are talking about a profession, besides the "what" we also have to consider the "how". So, let's begin by highlighting what it is that changes, and describe the new skills and knowledge that a new-generation art director should possess, aside from those inherited from his predecessors.

I'm not talking so much about technique. An art director may create the perfect TV advert without necessarily being an expert in film direction. That is, he should know enough about film direction without necessarily *being able* to be a film director. The art director behind the Red Bull campaign – the one with the matchstick man who manages to get out of all sorts of sticky situations thanks to the wings he's provided by the energy drink – does not necessarily know anything about animation techniques, nor does he necessarily know how to draw a tin can using a pencil. I may do, but that's beside the point. The point is that an art director does not have to be a technician, but he does have to have a knowledge of languages. And if it is true that the languages of today have evolved and multiplied, it is unthinkable that someone whose task is to ensure that everything is as it should be does not know anything about the codes, idioms and meanings of the world he lives in.

A good art director today should be capable, say, of supervising the *art direction* of an event in a town square. He should know how to dress the hostesses, how to arrange the stands and what music to choose. This does not mean that there shouldn't be any architects, set designers or professional DJs to handle these individual aspects too. But the greater the complexity of the affair and the necessity for specialist skills, the more important it is that the whole event be managed by a single figure. There should be one person who considers the whole thing globally and assures the commissioning client that what is being communicated within that context is exactly what the brand needs.

The same applies to a *smart mob*, for example. The people who get together to sing and dance or whatever all return to their respective homes afterwards. And what remains of the moment for those who were there? And, more importantly, for those who weren't? An image, a photograph, a video or an icon that should be able to convey meaning. That's the kind of job that calls for an art director, is it not? So why isn't a team of video-makers and photographers enough to create such an image? Because everything needs to be planned from the top. There has to be a clear image in mind before it even exists. Is a production designer necessary? Is a choreographer necessary? Are auditions for extras necessary? Well, these are the kinds of questions that today's art director should ask himself and be able to answer. And to do so, he must add to his cultural baggage several elements which, until a short time ago, he might have considered unnecessary or at least optional.

Here's one more example. In the beginning we talked about how the world of the web, drained by fleeing creatives (and art directors too), has been left in the hands of figures that are more like graphic artists and designers than art directors. Now that this leak has been forcibly stemmed by a market demand (and a clientele) that can no longer be ignored, art directors at long last have to study that subject too. Once again, I'm not asking for the study curricula of future creative directors to be crammed with Flash or Javascript programming courses. It is just that it has become important to understand and follow the development of the web's visual languages and to learn the difference between a portal and a landing page.

Ask any art director what the difference is between a single-page advertisement and a billboard. You'll find that he'll give you a precise answer. The single-page advertisement appears in a reading context, so if the inclusion of body copy proved useful, it could be done. In billboards body copy is a no-no: no-one can read more than two lines of text on a billboard as they race by trying to catch the traffic lights. And that's not all. Page layout rules also change, as do the "tricks" for catching the eye – choice of colour, lettering etc. (Of course, the truly great creatives are those who know how to break the rules, but generally before breaking them they study them in depth.)

Now ask any art director what the rules of layout are for a competition website. I doubt he will know. This is wrong; this is not contemporary thinking. In the new creative foursome there is no room for such an art director, just as it was impossible to imagine, in the old creative duo, an art director able to create a storyboard but not a poster layout.

One last practical case so that we understand each other. Once upon a time there were direct marketing agencies, and art directors knew perfectly well how to create the layout of a letter and how to design an envelope. Once upon a time there were promotional events agencies and they had their own graphics departments that were experts in creating small bubbles (and giant bubbles) in Day-Glo fuchsia and yellow. Once upon a time there were packaging agencies well versed in finding just the right position for the nutritional information tables required by law. Once upon a time there were agencies who handled visual merchandising and studied shop window design to promote the sale of the right products.

These agencies still exist today and possess specific, quasi-scientific skills, and it would be wrong to try and do away with them. However, at the same time today's advertising agencies are being asked to take into account all the above aspects during the creative design phase. Sometimes, through lack of sizeable budgets (since 2008 we have been in the throes of an unprecedented economic crisis), the only available medium is the shop window at sales outlets. At others, the only way to relaunch a brand is through a competition. And once again we witness how the future of an insurance company hangs on its ability to communicate its values and what it can offer its customers directly when they renew their policies (or allow them to expire, if they remain unconvinced by the company's communication). An agency today must be capable of handling such challenges if it doesn't wish to remain inside its anachronistic bunker, waiting for someone to ask it for a TV commercial and nothing else.

Now, one individual alone cannot possibly work singlehandedly at a high level on a mailing campaign, promo, packshot, site or TV commercial. It is true that Da Vinci – inventor, scientist, painter, sculptor – existed. It is true that the species evolves. However, let us try to keep our feet firmly on the ground here and not become delirious with sci-fi hypotheses.

Ruling out, therefore, the mandatory requisite of "genius" on the curriculum of an aspiring art director, we have to imagine the new art director as someone who knows how to answer the many important questions posed by the components of his quartet. Does this DEM (direct email) sent to the client's database have the correct layout? Yes, the art director said so. Is dimmed lighting during the event okay? Yes, the art director said so. Is it okay for the lettering on the competition postcard to be completely different from that of the campaign? No, the art director said so. How many suitcases should be placed in that bank shop window to attract the most attention? Two, the art director said so.

The kind of art director we need today is a supervisor (a competent one) to oversee all that goes into the *image* of a campaign, whatever its guise. He doesn't have to know how to do everything, but he should know how to liaise with film directors and photographers, as he always has done, as well as with architects, set designers, choreographers, web designers, the devisers of "mechanical" promotional schemes, brand designers, iPhone and iPad developers etc.

Some evolution is required; an evolution in complete continuity with what art directors always have done, only with a more open mind and a richer, more extensive database of skills. No small order, but things will be worse for his team-mates, as you'll soon see.

9

FRESH FROM THE STATES: THE IDEA WRITER

I had already written most of this chapter, giving a detailed account of the evolution of the copywriter, when I came across a very interesting book (in many aspects) that kept cropping up over and over again. What was most intriguing was its title: *The Idea Writers*. Subtitle: *Copywriting in a new media* and *marketing era*. Before throwing myself headlong into two hundred-odd pages of text I had succeeded in finding the definition (which had for weeks eluded me) to describe one of the four components of my creative team: *Idea Writer*. Sounds good.

I admit that for a moment I also thought it was bad news: someone before me had already defined the professional figure I was describing and I could not be the proud owner of the title of innovator (fictitious, but narcissistically gratifying). However, after the first few minutes of envying Teressa Iezzi, the writer and neologist, I got over it and instead focused on the positive side, or rather the two positive sides, of the issue.

The first: if an overseas opinion leader has thought what I thought, then maybe this chapter is significant; even though, fortunately, Ms Iezzi does not say exactly what I say (so plagiarism has been avoided).

The second positive aspect is that I, in spite of all my efforts, have been unable to arrive at such a precise conclusion. I circumvented it; I knew what I wanted to say, but I was never entirely satisfied with how I had worded it, because I knew that to be able to describe the latter-day copywriter I had to broaden his sphere of action without straying from his core: words. My shortlist of options before being struck along the road to Damascus was rather short. It wasn't the accurate, comprehensive synthesis of what I wanted to say.

My initial idea for an epithet was "Content Writer". Not that this was wrong, because to tell the truth, the concept of the evolution of the copywriter is definitely in the direction of content. Copywriting nowadays involves more than the mere drafting of text: it has to be devised. What we said about the art director in the previous chapter on the subject of the proliferation of media, situations and languages also, of course, applies to the copywriter.

Let's begin with an example: the campaign develops into an event. In this case, is the copywriter the one who writes the texts for the posters or else comes up with the title of the event? No siree. That's how it used to be, when events were mainly conventions or business activities or in any case important, but by no means strategic "accessories" in the communication economy of a brand. Today there are brands that communicate *solely* through their events. Go back and browse through the past, if you can. You will discover that the largest events agencies of the nineties and the noughties didn't just have a single copywriter. (Not even an art director, to tell the truth, but in the *visual* field they did at least have one good graphic artist plus architects and set directors.) It was completely different (do I have to say it again?).

Today events have become a viable (and frequent) means of brand-consumer communication, and as such require the same strategic-creative sensitivity which for years was the sole prerogative of *above the line*. So the copywriter has to have a central role. He must, first and foremost, be part of the definition of the creative idea.

And this, in the instance of an event, should answer the question: "what has to happen?". In other words: "what is the content of the event?". This is where the definition of the *Content Writer* comes in.

And not just for events. Let's consider a website, or more to the point, a social media project in which content really is everything. Let's think of one big neutral idea in a context like today's, where in order to have an audience one has to be interesting (no offence to Auditel, which until recently monitored a guaranteed passive audience). Here content certainly becomes a core part of business communication. To remain in symmetry with the redefinition of the art director, I'd say that today the copywriter is now "the writer".

Hence the title of *Content Writer* fits the bill. If I remain not entirely convinced and I abandon it along the way it will mainly be because of the risk of misunderstanding. The first image this definition conjures is not that of an author: it's that of a writer. The person who writes content could be the person who writes pages and pages of text for a magazine, a brochure or an internet site. Moreover, there's a great (and growing) demand for this type of content – less creative but with greater depth. Some organizations, mostly with a press office slant, are gearing themselves to providing a writing service for companies that – having elected to converse with their consumers – now find themselves saddled with the burden of always having to have something new to say and topics to address. Someone has to handle, create, write and propagate the content. It doesn't necessarily have to be a creative advertiser, so he's not our man.

After the option of Content Writer I assessed (and discarded straightaway) a second fascinating but entirely inappropriate title: “Conversation Writer”. This definition had a strong quality: it casts us straight into modernity, lining us up with statements that today are widely acknowledged: “markets are conversations” is the first of the 95 points of the *Cluetrain Manifesto*, which is still very much in vogue.

To the socio-ideological aspect we add the practical one, which is associated with the exponential growth of social networks that daily gain more ground in terms of work (and business) for communicators. So, *Conversation Writer* could be a very modern and, if you like, endearingly pandering way of describing the evolution of the role of the copywriter.

But – and there is a but – if it is true that, in an overall sense, this definition could work, in practice I feel the risks would outweigh the opportunities. The main risk is that the definition is restrictive with no room for scope. The literal meaning that people are likely to attribute to “conversation” limits its scope. One talks, the other listens, then replies, etc. A dialogue is an ongoing exchange that certainly rules out any idea of a TV commercial. Sure, I have a friend (his name is Rino and he’s a nice bloke, of course) who speaks to film actors, threatening the nasty ones and encouraging the nice ones. However, let’s just say I prefer to see him as the curious side of a special person rather than accept calling that kind of repartee a *conversation*. As regards the demagogy of “everything changes”, refuse to accept it –

one headline does not constitute a dialogue.

As with *Content Writer*, here too there is a risk of creating confusion. Today one of the professional figures most in demand at agencies is that of the *community manager* – the person who, well versed in the logic and language of the social media, handles the editorial planning (or conversational planning, obviously!), writes posts on the Facebook and Twitter profiles of companies, tones down pages and replies to comments with the main aim of animating exchanges and keeping the relationship alive.

I thought: if someone came to me telling me that he was a conversation writer, I would definitely imagine it to be a job of that kind. Which is not the one we are talking about here. The ability to converse is one of the points that should be included in the curriculum of the new-style copywriter, but this is only one aspect of his new job.

I also examined the possibility of being particularly *trenchant* and plumping for "Storyteller", which is just another way of saying that today advertising campaigns have to be able to communicate (through any medium) something that touches the public at large. Yet almost all the aforementioned objections applied to this too, even without taking into account the positive qualities of the modernity of the term.

In the end I found myself circling the word *idea*, which is very evocative in the creation trade. As a term, it is less technical and broader in meaning. I was taken with labels like “idea creator” or “idea thinker” or even “idea manager”. However, it is obvious that it’s a bit like saying “advertiser”, right? Before laying all his aesthetic tastes and flair for images on his team, the art director, as we so extensively reminded you earlier, acts both as a provider of ideas and a copy creator. So why limit the definition of his colleague to a producer of ideas? What is it that makes these two so different? If I had to explain all this to my youngest daughter (the eldest knows full well now), I would simplify things by saying that after having come up with an idea together, the art director is the one who designs it and the copywriter the one who writes it.

This is why when Mark Tungate told me he’d read Teresa Iezzi’s book, I realized that this time I would have to renounce my neologistic aspirations and surrender the labelling honour to my overseas friend: *Idea Writer* was exactly the concept I wished to express. Today’s copywriter is not just involved with script and body copy: he has to write ideas; “writing them” being the operative phrase. Ms Iezzi highlights this aspect by stating that “the explosion of creative opportunities does not exonerate the copywriter from the burden of having to face what the writer has had to face since time immemorial: the blank page.” As such, the copywriter’s new epithet cannot exclude his definition as a writer first and foremost.

It is the copywriter’s humanistic background, sensitivity and love of words that constitute the elements of perfect continuity with his predecessors. The content, on the other hand, changes (considerably).

Rob Reilly of the Crispin Porter + Bogusky agency even goes so far as to say that "copywriters are inventors". It is an attractive phrase, the kind that will enter aphorism anthologies. But, in my opinion, its limitation is that it's not applicable to creatives in general or better still to my new extended creative duo. Indeed, probably it is this very evolution (the kind that today requires more the approach and talent of an inventor than just a creative person) to create the conditions for the duo to become a foursome.

Remember Burger King's idea of the Whopper Sacrifice? Web-users were urged to "sacrifice a friend", that is to say, to remove a person from their list of friends on Facebook in order to receive for free in return one of the iconic hamburgers. Needless to say, it was a planetary success, to the point that although now old, it still remains one of the most cited examples in books like this. But here's the thing: it is an excellent example of what I mean by invention. Unfortunately, I was not on the creative team that spawned the idea, but I remain firmly convinced that there were several heads – all with different skills and degrees of sensitivity – behind the invention of that project, because there is a bit of everything in it: powerful strategic insight, an exceptional hi-tech solution, a powerful newsworthy concept and impeccable development.

What part will the copywriter have played? Once again:

I wasn't there and therefore cannot possibly know how the concept was developed. But I did come across a statement by Jeff Benjamin who highlights just what we were discussing on the subject of writing: "The writing in that case in particular was extremely important ... We revised the texts many times over. People thought, oh that's enough of doing things in which you get rid of your friends – but it had to be fun, not misinterpreted, it had to be clear what was meant to be done because many people find Facebook applications tricky. These are the kind of great challenges that a copywriter has to tackle."

Enthusiastic and knowledgeable, competent in many fields (added to the traditional ones of film and literature). Conversationalist and minstrel. Inventor and writer. This is the kind of Idea Writer needed by the new creative team of today.

10

THE ATTENTION PLANNER

Over these past few days (we're coming to the end of 2012) I've been reading a study on TV audiences. Amidst all the boring diatribes ("resistance" fighters vs. digital advertising supporters) and forecasts on the presumed end of TV as the advertising medium, there was one objective piece of data I found interesting, which was this: in Italy, generalist TV is steadily losing ground to digital networks (satellite and/or digital terrestrial) which today make up a whopping 30% of the share.

This means that today over a third of TV viewers can no longer be reached through planning with Rai or Media-set let's include La7 as well, the only generalist TV station on the rise). The solution for planners would seem to be an easy one: the budgets earmarked for one party should be assigned to another. And perhaps they would even save a little, given the growing competition.

But it's not quite like that. If buying advertising space on generalist stations means choosing from seven networks (the three belonging to Rai, and the three belonging to Media-set and La7), then on the digital terrestrial and satellite scene the question changes considerably. Limiting ourselves to the channels dealt with in official and certified reports, that makes 140. But if you turn on the TV and do a bit of channel hopping, you'll scroll the images of over 800 different channels. So, in theory, to show your TV advertisement to 30% or so of non-generalist TV viewers you would have to plan them all. And I'd like to see you do that.

Even if people continue to watch TV, the fragmentation of offer leads to a fragmentation in viewing figures. So add reaching a target and *delivering* a message to the list of difficulties for advertisers.

I began with TV, but the same applies to all media. The age-old certainties that "investment A" corresponds to "result B" are crumbling day by day. Many pretend that this is not so; many media centres and virtually all agencies are behaving as though nothing is wrong, producing one study after another to prove the unprovable. And many clients believe them (or at least pretend to) because otherwise they would be lost. How can they possibly make decisions without the GRP compass? Until someone has the courage to say "it's over", the usual route will remain the one to cling to if you want to avoid running risks.

Of course, it is true that at the end of the year these clients will come to realize all too well that people have not seen their communication (and so did not buy their products), but the tendency will be to blame the economic crisis, history and the inevitability of fate. After all, things are going badly for almost everyone at the moment, and this contributes a lot to assuaging the feeling of responsibility.

It is no coincidence that I've said that things are going badly for *almost* everyone: search the internet and you'll have no trouble in coming across some hugely successful examples of companies that are thriving in spite of this awful macroeconomic situation. How are they doing it? Is it all luck?

There are those who say that times of economic crisis are the ones in which greater investment should be made, because they are full of hidden opportunities. I say that one doesn't necessarily have to invest more, particularly if resources are scarce, but one should certainly invest more wisely; that is to say, not squander efforts or create messages that no-one will ever listen to. In other words: the best idea in the world is useless if no-one hears it. So the aim is to make sure that one's communication gets the right kind of exposure. But how does one go about achieving this result? Simple. With creativity.

My theory, therefore, is this: there are currently countless channels and places for reaching one's target. Data, studies and tools are all helpful in getting the problem into focus, but they cannot solve it. Finding the way to deliver one's message to a recipient is part of the creative side of the job. Besides, as Reeves said, "the art of advertising is getting a message into the heads of the most people at the lowest possible cost". Ensuring that an advertising idea can produce an audience is the task of a creative person. Finding the key to the door of our era's sharing attitude, and by doing so let the brand or product in, is the job of a creative person. Even choosing a target can be a creative task. However, one naïve question: who performs this specific creative task?

Monsieur de Lapalisse replies: a creative.

And so here comes the first of the new creatives running to the assistance of the art director and the copywriter. I've called him the *Attention Planner.* He is the one whose task within the creative team is to bring knowledge of the media (beginning with the semi-classics), public relations (from traditional to digital PR), events and the territory. And of people and the world. And then to use that knowledge to create ideas.

I know, it's all a little complicated to explain. It's not as it was for the art director and the copywriter, whose roles have simply *morphed*. This is a figure that does not exist anywhere. But it is also one who we shall soon be unable to do without. (I know, at this point my low profile style goes out of the window, but the *Attention Planner* really is the figure I see as the turning point and of whom I am most proud!)

If we really want to find him a predecessor then we could look to the figures abroad known as *communication planners* or *channel planners*, who in turn are evolved versions of *media planners*. The leap, however, is a giant one: the figure I speak of, although blessed with skills of that kind, has a decidedly creative mindset. Moreover, Paul Woolmington, founder of Naked Communications (one of the largest of the big new names in the world of advertising) also agrees: "In future being a great communication planner will be similar to being a great creative". Well, the future is now and the *Attention Planner* is to all intents and purposes a creative.

To better explain the role of this "superbeing", I'll try using a few helpful examples.

Let's start with a case history I am particularly familiar with, because it was created a couple of years ago by Now Available. For once we aren't bothering any international guru (we'll do it directly afterwards though, have no fear).

The client was Galbusera, and the name of the product was Tra, a semi-sweet snack for any time of the day (a rival of the better-known and richer Ritz and TUC brands, to put you in the picture). Galbusera's problem: poor sales, a continuation of which would have led to de-listing (in other words, they would have been "hounded off" supermarket shelves). The agency's challenge: to solve the client's problem on a seemingly meagre budget.

A great traditional creative idea was not going to be enough. A comprehensive campaign would be needed to hinge everything together: media, newsworthiness, "strategic" creativity and a fast-acting ability to sell (for the sword of Damocles threatened extinction).

Alas, the *Attention Planner* did not exist, so to get the job done a plethora of professional figures assembled around the table – classic art directors and copywriters, the media planner, the PR manager, the events manager, the strategic planner and the one we used to call the *unconventional planner*. Thanks to the effort required of everyone to think together without dividing the task in hand in the later stages (as was the custom), we came up with the solution.

Today I really cannot say which of the parties or which person was responsible for the winning idea. Maybe it came from Valentina's media mind: "The product does not have a clue moment, it can fit between one thing and another – as the name itself suggests – so let's turn this fact into a media idea with very short (and cheap) formats that can be 'slipped in' anywhere, with a chance of ending up on TV." Or perhaps the idea came from the creative director, Sergio: "Let's do a half-ad: a campaign that says 'A Tra fits in nicely between one ad and another'. Perhaps it could even have a jingle, so it will remain in people's minds more easily". Or maybe the idea came from the events expert, Michele: "Let's find a creative justification for the fact that we will distribute product samples all over the place. A Tra fits in nicely between one place and another. Tra are good, so if people try them, they'll buy them."

I really don't remember how it went, but the moral of the tale is clear: we created an "intrusive" campaign strategy in which the message and the means used to convey it were extremely coherent, thus bolstering one another. This led to a seven-second ad (complete with jingle) that was aired for fifteen days during prime-time on Mediaset, while the radio version was aired on Radio Deejay. At the same time, intensive sampling activities were carried out in different areas of a number of cities: "a Tra is just the ticket between stops" was the message used at underground and mainline train stations; "Tra in between meetings" at management centres; "between one shop window and another" along shopping avenues, etc. Then there was guerrilla marketing at hypermarkets: going up in the lift, for example, you would see tinystickers reading "you can fit a Tra in between one floor and another". And, of course, the Tra brand made its way onto Facebook and other social media networks as well.

The creative presentation to the client went down very well and as a result the campaign was purchased. It was not so much an idea for an ad campaign as the discovery of a communication strategy. It was .ot the kind of project that would have come from a media centre because at the heart of it all was a creative idea. In fact, it came from a creative agency, which, even so, would not hava been able to achieve that result had many heads with different fields of expertise not come together to produce a great idea. A very expensive exercise for an agency in terms of human resources, but the result repaid the effort: in the month following the campaign, Tra sales rose by 38% (Nielsen's word). So, there was no de-listing – on the contrary; the following year Galbusera introduced two new products, "Mini Tra" and "Tra Light". And the agency got the budget again, this time larger than that of the previous year.

This is the kind of work that clients increasingly expect from advertising agencies and that advertising agencies must therefore entrust to their creatives. And here we return to our original theory: can we really ask our old creative duo to learn all about the media, PR, events and promotions well enough to be able to include them in their daily thinking as they do for the film, TV, radio, press and, now, web industries? I say we can't, as you will have already understood. And I also say that the Attention Planner is without doubt the figure of the new creative that they will no longer be able to do without, and who they will welcome into their room as soon as they have the good fortune to run into one.

Let us continue with our job description of the *Attention Planner*, to explain his role and skills more clearly. For example, just as it is part of the art director's job to meet with film studios, film directors and photographers, so must the “attention creator” not shy away from meeting the media, getting around town and meeting with editors and journalists as well as with artists, musicians and architects. For his ideas originate from what he knows; from the possibilities he discovers or imagines and verifies each day. If one day someone discovers how to turn architectural landscape into advertising media (as was suggested to me by Mr Stefano Boeri, architect, in a conversation published in the monthly magazine Adv), that person will be an *Attention Planner*.

During a chat with Fox’s agency, for example, an *Attention Planner* might discover a willingness on their part to work together to create new TV formats (if a media clerk without the right creative disposition were to talk to Fox, they would probably end up going back home and waiting for the special events list to arrive; the *Attention Planner,* on the other hand, being a creative person, would go home and write to the agency with ten ideas he’d come up with in the car on the way home to sound out their feasibility).

Over an aperitif with the chief editor of Gazzetta dello Sport (and with a good idea already loaded in your barrel) you could find out if it would be possible to organize sporting-advertising events in a co-marketing venture with a view to achieving exceptional communication objectives.

And so on. Lateral thinking is *Attention Planner’s* warhorse, yet he is the most pragmatic of the creatives. He only offers the team feasible ideas, although ideally they’d have to be original ones that have never been done before via any means, be it TV, on the road, web, radio, or through ambient or cinema advertising.

Given that hunger is the best sauce, I shall tell you (briefly this time) about another case history from Now Available. I cannot give you the post-campaign data because, at the time of writing, the project is still to get underway. So you can be sure that I'm not using it to boast (I can't even tell you the name of the brand); it's only to give you yet another example of what an *Attention Planner* must and can do.

The brief is very demanding: working with a product that has two competitors that are decidedly stronger in terms of awareness, equity and consequently market share. The territory is that of the mass market: the food and drink sector. The available budget is below that of a decent TV commercial. Not even the invention of a strategy such as that of Tra could help.

The initial idea – positioning and differentiating the product – came from the copywriter. But it will be a press or billboard campaign, so it involves a *visual* and a *headline*. And if we'd planned on using traditional means, we'd manage two issues tops ... therefore it would be a completely futile exercise. However, the idea in itself is perfection, the kind that when you see it you cannot believe it's yours (if this has ever happened to you, you will know that feeling of proud awe).

So, what to do? How does one ensure that an idea conceived

in a traditional manner leads to something that will result in exposure? This is where our hero – the new Attention Planner – comes in, analyses the situation and says (given that this idea is for a billboard), let's do a billboard. Short on cash? Let's just do a single billboard. Then we'll make sure that everyone looks at that *single* billboard. How? By putting it in the right place (installing it in the main entrance hall of Milan's mainline station – this much I can tell you) and making it an object with which people on the web will want to interact in an all-new manner – nothing to do with QR codes or the like.

In this way many people, intrigued by the novelty, will want to try and interact with it (for example, they will want to see their picture on Facebook published in real-time on an illuminated board in a place where millions of people pass every day). The shyest can simply look at this billboard via the webcam, which will be streamed online 24/7. Who knows (the *Attention Planner* does – he's convinced of the fact because he has his contacts and knows who he's dealing with) if inviting a few journalists to the opening ceremony won't lead to a few lines in the press. And maybe even some TV exposure in the technology or fashion and style sections of programmes.

Then there are the bloggers who willingly lend space and visibility to good communication ideas. And the remaining budget, after having deducted production and rental costs at the station, we'll invest in buying traffic online, on

Facebook, on Google and on the sites most used by the target (but here we'll enlist the help of a media planner, for this is a job in itself and is more for a technician than a creative person).

I'm sorry I'm unable to give you more details, but I really cannot. I will however in the second edition of the book, when you will have told your friends to buy thousands of copies so that the publisher will be obliged to reprint it. Anyway, I hope you've got the gist of the idea.

Don't get me wrong: if in this case the *Attention Planner* came into play upon completion of the campaign, that is to say after a more *traditional* creative approach, it doesn't mean that this is the right model. Neither illude yourselves that the type of contribution he made could have come from a classic *media planner.* That's not how it happened: the media play their part, of course, but at the root of it all is the *creative idea* of creating a single billboard and turning part of it into an application to be propagated via the web. Installing a fixed webcam (with everything else going on behind it) is a creative idea. The name of the initiative (which helps its media appeal) is a creative idea. If he hadn't *roughly* known the cost of the space in Milan Central Station, if he hadn't known someone who could turn a poster into a giant interactive installation, then maybe the *Attention Planner* would not have had this idea. Yet his technical expertise (I'll say it for the last time) forms an important part of the all-essential cultural baggage targeted at a generation with certain ideas. Creative ones. Full stop.

I'd like to close this chapter with a flourish in the form of an anecdote on a famous campaign by the most legendary advertiser of our times. Perhaps you have heard of him: the client was Ecko, an *underground* American clothing brand that got the world talking. The agency was David Droga's. The creative brief asked for the brand to be brought closer to its urban nature: the founder is a graffiti artist and the street is the DNA of his brand. Provocative and sassy.

These were the elements on the table, along with a sizeable budget, but not one large enough for the production and broadcast of a Superbowl advertisement.

Solution: to "graffiti" the brand's message in a location affording maximum exposure. Why not the fuselage of Air Force One, the airplane of the President of the United States of America, probably the most protected transport means on the planet? Getting past all the Pentagon's security armed with spray cans was certainly a good way of drawing attention. It would lead to the appearance on the web and all America's main news bulletins of images of the outrageous prank. America's security was at risk. But the Pentagon denied it, claiming that the images were false.

People, however, continued to believe it and to forward the video to their friends. Upon the third denial from the Pentagon the hoax was revealed: it was a fake, albeit a superbly executed one. It was an advertising gimmick. The summary of the case history on the *Droga* 5 agency website talks about these pranks: over 100 showings by major TV stations; over 17,000 articles about it in on and offline publications worldwide; a total audience of 115 million; a documentary made by an American TV network. Three denials by the Pentagon. Average budget: zero bucks.

(A warning to clients: average budget zero, but the creative and production costs for an operation of that kind is necessarily very high. Do not go to your advertising agency asking for something similar with a budget of just 50,000 Euro!)

Droga 5 certainly didn't have an *Attention Planner* (I hadn't invented the figure yet), but there is no doubt that the creatives on the team were well versed in thinking outside of the box. And there is no doubt whatsoever that for the creation of a campaign of that kind the contribution of a creative with the vision and skill we have studied in these pages could come in handy.

The great final question remains: where do we dig out a creative person like this? Is there one on the market? No, I don't think so. At least not as complete as we would like. But he does not exist just as the art directors did not exist (in the beginning, as Mark Tungate teaches us in his *Adland*, there were artists, graphic artists and layout artists, but no art directors). The figure did not exist just as snowboarders didn't exist. Then the need arose, so they appeared. They came into being. First they appeared on the field. Then in schools. The same has to happen in this case. It is necessary to identify the figures who, either for what they do today or for their mental make-up (innate creativity and curiosity for the media world), come close to the textbook definition of the *Attention Planner*. This is their starting point for the final transformation.

11

THE DIGITAL CREATIVE PLANNER

Once again, the word "planner" appears in the job title of a creative, but a distinction needs to be made. In the instance of the Attention Planner, the word is used in its literal sense in reference to "he who plans with care", and in this particular instance, "he who is capable of finding the right creative solution to attract the target's attention".

In the instance of the Digital Creative Planner, however, the term should be interpreted using the meaning it has acquired in agency jargon. "The Planner" is a precise (more or less, and in any case we devoted an entire chapter to it) professional figure who is involved in strategy.

So the correct way to interpret this neologism is, according to the intentions of the author, something along the lines of Digital (adjective) Creative-Strategist (double noun).

Let's start with the adjective: this is a digital creative person. Definitely the most digital of the foursome. I don't think it is necessary, but I will say it once more: in this context, when I speak of digital I'm not necessarily thinking about the web or technology, but of a way of interpreting the world. A language that places sharing, participation, exchange and an absence of pontification at the centre of its grammar. The Digital Creative Planner is a network inhabitant, an assiduous, skilled habitué of blogs (beginning with his own), and an anticipator of trends. If a social network is about to be born, he will know. If the biggest flash mob in history is being organized, he will know. If a company is redefining its communication strategies with a view to listening to its consumers more, he will know.

He downloads all the iPhone and iPad apps, he loves them as a user, he studies them as a pro. And he dreams of being the next millionaire inventor of the app that the entire world will download. Not the one who will programme it (after all, he's no technician), but the one who will invent it (after all, he is a creative person).

He is well aware of what digital natives like because he is always in contact with them and their opinion leaders (even if these are not all natives). He takes part in workshops, bar-camps and anything else that can stimulate him and provide him with vision.

Thanks to his sensitivity and his haunts he is constantly

able to glean new insights, which are what he bases his ideas on. This is why I refer to him as a creative planner: the output he generates is a creative idea. Yet behind the scenes there is always a digital dictionary and a precise insight that guides his strategic thought.

Well, this time I believe that in spite of the novelty of the character, his traits are quite clear and easy to explain. But when and how does a Digital Creative Planner become necessary in addressing a client's creative brief? The correct answer is: always.

Always, for even in a campaign studied using ultra-traditional means, one cannot ignore context. We discussed this several chapters ago. We are in the post-digital age in which the term "post" does not mean that digital is behind us, but the exact opposite: in light of the digital explosion as an epoch-making event, today we live in an era that is inevitably influenced by that event.

One note: unlike the Attention Planner, the Digital Creative Planner already exists at some agencies, even though he still doesn't know that this is his title, so he introduces himself under a false name. This is why it is a little difficult to provide practical examples of his work with a view to demonstrating the kind of contribution one may expect from him.

Let's begin with a case where his influence is particularly manifest. Back in 2008, the direct insurance firm Zuritel decided to change its name to Zurich Connect. The client wanted this rebranding to be talked about on the internet ... no easy task (who would be interested in a Swiss insurance company changing its name?). What is it that attracts people online? What could encourage the word-of-mouth advertising requested in the creative brief? What could be latched onto? The first idea was: let's make a fake, because fakes attract digital media and network plague-spreaders (we all know what a fake is now, but back in 2008 it was not so obvious). Okay, but what kind of falsehood do we have to come up with that connects with our brand message?

And so the creative task begins: Digital Creative Planner (who wasn't called that at the time) together with the art director and copywriter.

The idea that came up was this: let's launch the first-ever car hologram: a box installed in a car that makes a semi-transparent figure appear in the passenger seat who can help the driver in different ways, particularly in ensuring his safety in the instance of problems. Ten demo videos were produced showing how to install and operate it. The direction was the classic kind used for low-budget industrial films. The hologram, however, was worthy of special effects cinema.

The endorser spoke in English (but was Asian, because the fake manufacturing firm was the Wu Ming Corporation), supported by loosely translated subtitles. A website badly translated into Italian provided all the technical data and instructions for use.

The dominion was Swiss-registered (the hypothetical importer was Swiss, just like Zurich Connect). Its name contained useful elements for a future revelation: DA Connect (Driver Assistant Connect, as in Zurich Connect). A perfectly suitable payoff both for an assistant hologram of the future and a car insurance firm: "Safety First". A promise: the details on the distribution and sale of the innovative device would be revealed on 13 October (the official rebranding date). Leave your email address for a chance to win a trip to China (while we're at it), homeland of the prodigious DA Connect company.

And so the campaign was launched with seeding on YouTube, Google advertising, digital PR and press releases. Results soon followed. Repubblica TV (the main Italian daily news site) placed the demo videos on its homepage. Visibility on social networks went viral, as did the suspicion that it was all a hoax. The world's blogs and sites asked themselves: "Is it real?". It didn't take them long to work out that although carefully orchestrated, it was nevertheless a fake. The New York Times (yes, you did read correctly: The New York Times!) wrote to the agency asking for details to do a write-up on the case history in its marketing and communication section. And in its special feature on technology, corriere.it used the title: "A great fake goes wild on the web". And it asked: who is behind it?

The day of the reply. The homepage of the hologram's

website changes under the very eyes of the user with an animation that reveals the hoax: the DA Connect logo becomes Zurich Connect, and a piece of text (drafted by a good copywriter) comments: you don't need a hologram to be safe in your own car: all you need is a good insurance policy.

The creative idea is both interesting and original, but it would not have generated so much interest if there hadn't been such shrewd and digitally skilled (creative) direction. It wouldn't have taken much to turn intuition into a not very viral advertisement, or to change a hoax into an operation with the power to tweak the susceptibility of the most avid web-users (those who speak well or badly of a brand, who influence its "web reputation" which is often the reputation). Instead, the creative team was guided by the right person, someone who knew who he was dealing with because he frequents them at close quarters, someone who knew what was cool and what wasn't, which words to use and which to avoid, and how to think of and package an idea to make it net-friendly and so foster its success.

Now I'll step outside my own back yard to tell you about another case history not by Now Available. The preamble is the usual: what I know, I know through being an enthusiastic, attentive user, but I am ignorant as to how things behind the scenes actually developed.

We're in Korea. Tesco, the brand leader in large-scale distribution in Korea, is on the territory, while the Home Plus brand is only "number two". The creative brief for its agency therefore was to discover how communication could help the company improve its figures and get closer to its competitor, which had a greater number of sales outlets.

The solution? A billboard. You're kidding. And what does a billboard have to do with the chapter on the Digital Creative Planner? I'll explain, then you can see for yourself.

The gargantuan billboard, positioned in an underground tunnel, is a full-size photographic reproduction of the shelves of a Home Plus sales outlet with all the products arranged in a neat display. The invitation of the headline is explicit: use your smartphone to do the shopping. Right here, right now. Search among the shelves for the product you need, then train your phone on the QR code and you will find it in your virtual shopping trolley. Once you have chosen your products all you have to do is enter your credit card details, contact address and the shopping is done. (For the less digitalized among you, QR (Quick Response) codes are those ethnic-looking barcodes which, when photographed with a mobile phone, lead to a site or an application.) In actual fact, that billboard has become a veritable sales outlet, a very handy convenience store because it is literally in your street. No parking problems, no queues at the checkout.

However, the extraordinary thing is that such a tactical action and explicitly direct response approach was at the same time a great piece of branding; it was extremely newsworthy (it is no coincidence that this case history circled the world and chalked up many a creative award) and was highly successful in positioning the Home Plus brand as cool, innovative and on its customers' side.

In that case, was there a Digital Creative Planner? I don't know for sure – I wasn't there, and if I was, I was asleep, and yet I'm convinced that a figure of that type (whatever his stage name is in Korea) must have had a hand in it. Or better still, let's put it this way: in order to produce a campaign like that here in Italy today, the creative duo could not have done without a Digital Creative Planner. Campaigns like that are the ones that will restore meaning and value to advertising, and I'm ready to be in on it.

12

THE CONSUMER TURNS BRAINSTORMER: THE "CREATIVE CONSUMER"

I've already stuck my neck out in the previous chapters by saying that, to me, certain phrases like "it's the consumers who create communication" are the great demagogic discoveries which, if taken literally, contain more hypocrisy than modernity. However, this is not to say that the consumer (I'll continue to refer to him as such, without fear of offending anyone) really doesn't have a different, less passive role today. Much in the same way,

I've already stuck my neck out in the previous chapters by saying that, to me, certain phrases like "it's the consumers who create communication" are the great demagogic discoveries which, if taken literally, contain more hypocrisy than modernity. However, this is not to say that the consumer (I'll continue to refer to him as such, without fear of offending anyone) really doesn't have a different, less passive role today. Much in the same way, the voter, the TV viewer or the football fan potentially all have a different role. Compared to the past, they are different, but moreover they are knowledgeable and open to participation.

So, why not get consumers more involved in the creative process? Maybe you have heard all about *crowdsourcing*, where people online are hired to take part collectively in the creation of a project. On Wikipedia the etymology of the term is specified. It comes from *crowd* (common people) and *outsourcing* (the externalization of some of one's activities). In Italy, several companies have promoted activities like this, from "My kind of windmill" by Barilla to "Do you know how I see it?", the online building site for the construction, together with mums (and dads), of the future Nesquik website. Plus many more.

All these experiments have been successful, because besides obtaining invaluable suggestions from people, they also help companies show that they really are open to listening. They ask those who wish to help and they accept that people's opinions might be different from their own. A project like this is very modern and in terms of image it helps give the brand a face-lift for the future. Then, if we want to look at it from a more marketing-oriented point of view, it is obvious that if I create a product based on my consumers' instructions then those consumers will be more likely to buy it.

The other side of the *crowdsourcing* coin is often the numbers involved. I said so several chapters ago on the subject (contested by me) of the definition of the *Consumer Control Era*. Remember: just because it is possible to call in on the radio to ask for a dedication or comment on something – opportunities with age-old roots – it is not necessarily an indication that all Italians spend their time calling DJs on air.

The statistics confirm this theory, even as regards the internet. Anyone can have their say, but only a small percentage do. This percentage is even smaller if the number examined is not restricted to the number of internet users and takes into account the entire population. Did you know that in Italy around 30% of the population (limiting ourselves to the 16-74 age bracket) has never used the internet? This statistic appeared in the last survey by Censis in 2011. This is why *crowdsourcing* projects, at least those done to date, have more clout when it comes to building image, reputation and attention – if any – on the part of the media, rather than in that of advertising.

Sometimes behind crowdsourcing projects you will find focus group logic rather than real co-creation. Etymologically speaking, "co-creation" is about the simple division between users; but at times practice contradicts grammar, and one may often happen to run into initiatives that aim to create expert panels on which to test (or with which to choose) a communication, packaging, product or service idea. Long may these types of activity live and may they continue to be intelligent, useful and creative.

As for us, however, the *Creative Consumer* who complements the creative quartet – from the outside – distances us a little from this territory. Here we're talking about an individual who is called on to co-create live with no web mediation.

The aim is to introduce an element into the creative team during the idea generation phase that can bring a viewpoint which, in all likelihood, would otherwise have been lacking entirely: that of the product expert. We have already said this several times over, even when discussing the importance of planning and the creative brief: a great idea often comes from in-depth knowledge of the product and provides an insight that will touch a note with its devotees.

Imagine having to devise an ad campaign for a sports drink. Target: runners of all ages and social extraction, united by a passion for miles and miles of running. Now imagine that first moment, when the white page is still blank and the marker board untouched. There ensues an explosion of ideas, no holds barred, no criticism and no censure (the rules of brainstorming are great in this respect). Anything goes, because an imperfect or even totally wrong idea may lead to a better one, and so on and so forth.

Here I ask myself: among all these people present at this time could there not be an expert on the product, someone who knows more about it than others? And if there is competence, is it not the product of personal impassioned experience as opposed to study at the drawing board?

A runner, in our example: one of those who leaves the house at the crack of dawn with shorts and iPod (regardless of the temperature) to slip into one of the city's parks frequented by like-minded beings. Someone who, after a shower, will go back to being a manager, labourer, clerk or barman. And it matters not whether he aspires to win the New York marathon or to qualify for the cross-country school run. What matters is that he is useful for our cause, that running is his passion, and that he feels part of a community (in short, that from time to time he speaks in the first person plural, saying "we runners". Include a runner in the brainstorming phase for an isotonic drink and you'll see that he will be a great help in generating ideas. I am sure of it (and I have empirical proof to back it up).

The principle, therefore, is this: in an era where knowledge and a desire to join in are the characteristics that today's consumers have in common (because of this they are sometimes nicknamed *consumactors*), it is fitting and useful that the brands involve them in some way in the generation of their campaigns. However, this does not necessarily mean assigning them the responsibility of being the authors of communication. A few pages ago I polemicized about the rhetorical phrase "it's the consumers who create communication", so we know what we are talking about. We will not abandon our consumer ally.

Here is my proposal: in each brainstorming process, select an expert consumer and pay him as you would a creative freelancer – by doing so you are turning him into a brainstormer. Bring him into the agency, give him a computer and a desk and have him take part in the first creative meetings with the creative foursome. And as he is being asked for a professional contribution, pay him for the hours he works.

Of course, for the Creative Consumer's contribution to be truly interesting, the person chosen has to be the right one. What characteristics should one look for and how does one identify them?

First of all, let's clear the field of all possible misunderstandings. The Creative Consumer is *not* an element upon which to test creative ideas directly. The efficacy of *focus groups* is already highly questionable, given the difficulty of representing an often broad and heterogeneous target using such a small group. Imagine using a single individual as a spokesperson for an entire category. Besides being devoid of any statistical value it might lead to some awful howlers.

For the same reasons one could not think of using a brainstormer as a bringer of shared insights. He's a runner, but he is only one of millions. His needs are not necessarily those of his fellow enthusiasts. When he starts working with the creative team, the Creative Consumer isn't meant to represent anyone: once he steps across the agency's doorstep his sole task is to generate communication ideas.

So, here is the "identikit" of the Creative Consumer:

- he's an enthusiast and an expert with direct first-hand experience. He may be an expert in a particular field (running, for example) or in a category of products (such as luxury watches), or he may have direct experience with a product or brand (Samsung smartphones, for example)
- he's good at sharing – this is why he talks of his passion with his friends and colleagues and listens to their opinions and points of view; the experiences of others enrich his own
- he has creative aptitude, he likes advertising (in all its forms) and he's not afraid to speak his mind
- he has a sound cultural base and is curious and intelligent.

How do you go about recruiting him? By collecting candidates via a website and sifting through the profiles each time a "position becomes vacant". We at the agency have already started: www.brainstormer.it features a site constructed exactly like a recruiting portal. The general characteristics of the brainstormer are shown and all candidates are asked to categorize themselves according to their interests and passions (this they can do using a standard questionnaire).

In this way a database of potential brainstormers can be created and they can be contacted if and when the agency receives a job that suits them. Besides the form for spontaneous candidates, open to any profile and interest, vacant positions are also posted on the site as they arise. In this instance the description of the ideal candidate is very explicit and detailed, and preferential criteria are given for the selection, the period of collaboration and the fee envisaged. Let's be clear here: we're not creating millions of jobs and we won't make anyone rich. It may seem ambitious, but we think we can create the professional category of brainstormers. However, this does not mean that this period of Creative Consumers isn't valuable and, therefore, it is a justifiable expense.

So the team is complete. The fantastic four, together with "the twelfth player" (to use a football metaphor) are ready and warmed up; ready to take on the future of advertising.

PART IV THE END

13

LONG LIVE (NEUTRAL) ADVERTISING!

I want to keep on (or go back to) calling it advertising: that age-old, fascinating subject which, since time immemorial, has helped brands become big and companies achieve business success through strategy and creativity.

Today, in order to distance ourselves from outdated models, we tend to look for synonyms or alternatives. Advertising agencies no longer exist, but there has been a proliferation of communication agencies, digital agencies, marketing agencies and consulting agencies. The few agencies that still retain the word *advertising* in their names have inherited it from a past that they tend to repudiate.

Or (in a few rare cases, fortunately) nostalgically and anachronistically flatter.

It is my ambition, however, to champion the relaunch of advertising, recovering its appeal, values, sense and efficacy. No client today would wish for the birth of a "TVC Agency" (TVC standing for TV Commercials), but good advertising agencies are needed now just as much as they were yesterday, and perhaps even more so.

Those who say things like "today's advertising doesn't work anymore" have not understood what advertising is about, and probably don't even know its etymology or history. However, we should by now have understood one another. The advertising I speak of is the art of convincing people to prefer one brand or product over another by means of a creative campaign. I think that this, in terms of concept, is modern.

It is true that advertising today is very hard, but this is not a good reason for beating a retreat. On the contrary; as is always the case, opportunities often lurk within difficulties.

Today advertisers (and creatives on the front line) face an enormous challenge, but they also have the chance to invent something truly innovative, to communicate with their targets and to find themselves before a public that may be willing to be a part of and share their ideas. They have only to realize this and act accordingly by refusing to remain on their backsides sitting out the storm, waiting for it to pass.

I've indicated one of the possible ways in which this

profession could evolve which envisages the birth (and consolidation) of several new professional figures, which to my mind are essential. But for this to really take off, the push for change has to come from several fronts. From creative directors, for example, who are still too much like the "EACRs" I described in the Portraits chapter.

Nancy Vonk, co-chief creative officer of Ogilvy Toronto (quoted by Ms Iezzi) explains very well what a new generation creative director should ask his team for, by encouraging, or rather expecting, what I call *neutral thought*: "[creatives] should think of themselves as problem solvers, not ad makers. Ideally, begin every assignment looking directly at the business problem (or opportunity) and push it up with media-neutral thinking. If a client has asked for a print ad or banner ad or whatever specific medium, ignore that and look for a big idea. A great idea that truly solves the problem can be channelled into that print ad, etc. The client will see the specific medium they requested, but in the context of a holistic solution that can potentially inform many spaces."

Ms Vonk continues: "You use a very different lens if you're hunting for a TV spot (okay, so I have just 30 seconds to tell a story, here's the kind of short story I can tell) versus looking for a solution that could be literally anything. I tell people they aren't allowed to show me a TV script in the first round of ideas, if that's what the client asked for. Recently a team proposed a bake shop when a print ad was asked for.

The print ad happened, but it was one small component of a totally unexpected, refreshing solution."

I've reproduced Ms Vonk's thoughts word for word because she expresses perfectly the spirit that should drive the creative directors of tomorrow, if they want to be able to guide and manage our extended duos.

However, it's not just about guiding and managing: we are in the midst of major change, and the first challenge for creative directors is that of identifying and creating new figures.

Here, the help of *official* trainers might be useful: I remain utterly convinced that new study paths will have to be devised to replace current ones in order to prepare youngsters for a profession that no longer exists. It is time that schools stop placing aspiring creative youngsters before a "do you want to be an art director or a copywriter?" crossroads and bring their most suitable proposals in line with the times.

Italy has begun to import a little culture from abroad – the source I have been forced to use for all my quotations – for what I describe as the future is often already a reality outside Italy. The creatives who win the most interesting awards are not Italian. The awards are created abroad as well.

Meanwhile in Italy, we continue to add categories to further fragment our insignificant awards – for years now the Cannes Film Festival has been pushing us towards the amelioration of new-generation advertising. Just think of the Titanium Integrated Lion, which at long last is assuming the prestige of the *Film Lion* – is this not "stuff" for our fantastic four?

Come on, then, let's give it a try. Let's get creating and let's launch new creatives and a new way of doing advertising; and let's go back to calling it advertising without feeling old. Let us innovate, let us generate new campaigns that people will sit up for, listen to and remember. Let's help our clients to generate business through communication.

Lending trust and courage to our profession lies with us alone; it relies on our ability to invent and our creativity.

I very much like to think that we can do it.

Hands up if you want to play with me.

ACKNOWLEDGEMENTS

I have discovered that many readers skip the acknowledgements pages that often feature in books, be they essays or novels. I, however, always read them and am almost always satisfied. This is why, when it's my turn, I take it seriously.

I'll start with my thanks to Mark Tungate, the special guest in this book, who gave me its preface, his advice (imparted in a way worthy of any novel – at the Café Livre in Paris) and his respect. This man writes for Campaign and for The Times, he writes bestsellers that have been translated and sold worldwide, and yet when I told him about my idea and asked him for a contribution he said (honest!): "I would be honoured to write the preface".

I'd like to thank my two partners Stefano and Alessia, who gave me their support in the form of trust as well as many ideas which – as is my habit, but they've got used to it – I took and made my own in this book. Thanks also for taking on extra work (loads) when I was too busy with the world's chief systems to make my daily contribution to Now Available.

Additional thanks to Alessia, a careful reader and consultant, who went through every page of my manuscript, and who, besides having to put up with me in the office, also puts up with me in our private life. Thanks to her too for pretending not to be bored during all those weekends of my "retreat" from the outside world during which I wrote without speaking a word to her, apart from in the evenings over a much-deserved dinner. (Okay, I'll say it: thanks for the book title as well; the anonymous writer of the phrase "the creative couple is a foursome" was her.)

Thanks to my two daughters, Alice and Viola, who were also forced to sacrifice hours they might have spent with Dad and petitioned instead to "leave me alone" and "play over there" in order to allow me to meet the deadlines set by my publisher.

Thanks to Ross, the Digital Creative Planner ante *litteram* who, besides being a constant stimulus for my attention to the "truest" social and digital networks, is the one who deserves almost all the credit for the idea of brainstormers. And I'm almost admitting that only to keep the burden of any criticism to myself, while leaving all the honour and praise for her.

The entire agency cannot end up on the acknowledgements page, but it is thanks to the support and contribution of all my friends and colleagues that I have never lost the will to do things, to think, to create and to write.

In particular I wish to thank Tina and Alessandra who, besides offering moral support, also gave me essential practical help with aspects of art direction and layout. What's more, Tina is the one who found the English title for this book: the idea of the Creative 4Cast comes from her creative mind.

Thanks to all the great advertisers, past and present, for their inspiration, examples and quotations that I have had the gall to use here to support my theories. They will never know that they were cited and thanked, but it feels right to have done so anyway.

Thanks also to the advertisers of the future: the future of this book will depend on how much they come to resemble my four champions. I am counting on you (and I refer in particular to the three or four candidates currently at Now Available; they know very well that they are the preordained ones).

My thanks to Laura Deambrogio, who hasn't even read this book (she probably doesn't even remember that it is coming out), but who was a great help in writing the first one, *Not Available*. Since that time I have never thanked her publicly so, a few years down the line, I'm doing so now. The reason for thanking her, however, has not expired:

without the first book there could not have been a second.

And lastly, my thanks to Martin Liu who accepted to have my book translated and to promote its English version (published in Italy by Fausto Lupetti), and thanks also to all you adventurous readers who embarked on a journey with me through the pages of my book, right to the very last line.

Until next time. Curtain.